M000307641

You Build a Business with

People

Eric M. Johnson

ISBN 978-0-9894312-0-0

Contents

Foreword

The story of E.P. Arnold and Arnold Motor Supply is a fascinating story because it is made up of fascinating people. It would not have been possible to set down this narrative without firsthand accounts from so many of those who worked for the company over the years. I was extremely fortunate to have lengthy and enjoyable conversations with Mr. Arnold's first employee, Mrs. Florence Rusch who gave me invaluable insight into the first decades of the company and without her this story could not have been retold.

Joyce Wagner joined the company in 1950 and stayed for the entire second half of the twentieth century. Her knowledge of the company and her relationship with the Arnold family are irreplaceable. In addition to Florence and Joyce, I spoke with many current and retired partners who each contributed to the overall picture of the company.

Many people across the city of Spencer have been helpful in gathering research; especially the librarians at the Spencer Public Library, the staff at the Parker Historical Society, Spencer Planning Director Kirby Schmidt, and the staff at the Clay County Auditor and Recorder Offices. Rick Krebsbach of Marvin Burk Photography has provided many of the photographs used throughout.

1. American Dream

This is the story of an American Dream; the story of an entrepreneur and the business he built through the Roaring Twenties, the Great Depression, through the Second World War, and the Post War Boom. Just what is this American Dream? Ask twenty people to define the Dream, and you will likely get twenty different answers, some idealistic, some cynical, most somewhere in between. Some will refer to our Declaration of Independence and say the American Dream is life, liberty, and the pursuit of happiness. Others go farther and say the American Dream is about obtaining wealth and belongings or living a certain kind of life. Most definitions will include concepts like Perseverance, Hard Work, Freedom, Success, Equality and Opportunity.

In his book *The Comeback*, Gary Shapiro defines the American dream this way: "Work hard in our free society, and your children will have the opportunity for a better life than you had." Of course, not everyone loves this dream. Some believe the American Dream to be a nightmare of greed and avarice. Some Americans, though they hear of it constantly, have no notion of what the American Dream really is. Politicians love to evoke it in their speeches and most of us think it is a good thing to pursue. The reality is, we can't come to agreement on how to define that ever elusive American Dream. In the 21st century, some doubt this great dream still even exists at all.

Of course there is no right or wrong answer. Each person is free to dream their own dream, which of course is what makes the American Dream so powerful. An informal survey revealed the following definitions:

> The American Dream is the belief that this country affords all its citizens the opportunity to go as far as their ambition, intellect, and talent will take them. The opportunity, not the guarantee, to achieve success however we personally define it.

> Life, liberty, and the PURSUIT of happiness (the happiness part is not guaranteed).

> Owning your own house

> Life of material comfort and happiness

> Having the freedom to strive for a better life through hard work

> Personal freedom, the pursuit of happiness, and building the life you choose.

> Freedom and security to do the things you enjoy.

> To see your children have an education and career choices beyond your own.

> Freedom of Speech, Freedom of Worship,
> Freedom from Want, Freedom from Fear (The
> Four Freedoms as painted by Norman
> Rockwell.)

James Truslow Adams is the man credited with coining the phrase "American Dream." Adams was a well-known American historian and author who lived from 1878 until 1949. The dawn of the twentieth century was an amazing time of transition and heady optimism in America, a time when the American Dream was definitely alive and well, and Adams was there to document it. In his *The Epic of America*, published in 1931, he describes life this way: "In America, as contrasted with Europe, it was open to every man, theoretically at least, to rise from the very bottom to the top." For Adams and his early twentieth century contemporaries, the American Dream was about potential.

In the paragraph that defined this dream, Adams went on to say, "that dream of a land in which life should be better and richer and fuller for every man, with opportunity for each according to his ability or achievement. It is a difficult dream for the European upper classes to interpret adequately, and too many of us ourselves have grown weary and mistrustful of it. It is not a dream of motor cars and high wages merely, but a dream of social order in which each man and each woman shall be able to attain to the fullest stature of which they are innately capable, and be recognized by others for what they are, regardless of the fortuitous circumstances of birth or position."

Perhaps no contemporary of Adams' was better at putting thoughts about this nation into words than Mark Twain. His novel, *The Gilded Age,* was written in 1873 in collaboration with his friend and neighbor Charles Dudley Warner. The novel is a commentary on post-Civil War America and proves to be prophetic of the direction the nation would follow in the years after it was written. In his preface, Twain, described the work this way: "In America nearly every man has his dream, his pet scheme, whereby he is to advance himself socially or pecuniarily. It is this all-pervading speculativeness which we tried to illustrate in 'The Gilded Age'. It is a characteristic which is both bad and good, for both the individual and the nation. Good, because it allows neither to stand still, but drives both for ever on, towards some point or other which is ahead, not behind nor at one side. Bad, because the chosen point is often badly chosen, and then the individual is wrecked; the aggregations of such cases affects the nation, and so is bad for the nation. Still, it is a trait which is of course better for a people to have and sometimes suffer from than to be without."

This Gilded Age which saw the nation advance from the Civil War to the dawn of the Twentieth Century was a time of rapid growth and enormous immigration, as people from other parts of the world saw the American Dream providing potential they could never achieve in their homelands. Ellis Island was opened in 1892 to accommodate the waves of immigrants coming to America from Europe in pursuit of the promised opportunity.

Railroads and industrialization created personal fortunes during the Gilded Age, the likes of which were never seen before in the United States, nor have been seen since. Though many of these captains of industry were philanthropic with their vast fortunes, the unfair nature of the monopolies they created to gain their wealth resulted in the need for new antitrust legislation to curb the anti-competitive business practices of the day. The Sherman Act was passed in 1890 in order to "protect the consumers by preventing arrangements designed, or which tend, to advance the cost of goods to the consumer."

Both Adams and Twain wrote about an America still young and untamed enough that almost anything could happen. It was a more dangerous, adventurous America with higher peaks and lower valleys. It was in this America that the Dream was born. Those who take a shallow look at only the surface of the American Dream see merely wealth. Adams was careful to point out that while "high wages" may be a motivation for and a result of the dream, the dream itself is much deeper. It is really the freedom to go as far as an individual's talent and work ethic will allow.

Unfortunately, in order to truly be free to succeed, one must also be free to fail, a reality not lost on the innovators and entrepreneurs of Adams' time. Looking back from a century later in a time of government bailouts and safety nets, it is difficult to understand what life was like for these Americans. We are, however, well aware of many of the great business successes from the dawn of the

13

Twentieth Century: successes who are now household names.

Americans today who have never heard of Harvey Firestone have certainly heard of his tire company. Ask someone how William Wrigley became wealthy and they will likely guess chewing gum. Joining Firestone and Wrigley during this age of innovation are notables like George Eastman whose Kodak company brought photography to the masses, and Guglielmo Marconi who pioneered radio. Of course this was also the time of internal combustion engines and powered flight, as Henry Ford and the Wright Brothers both made history. Those big success stories from the dawn of the Twentieth Century are all a part of today's lexicon.

This American Dream, however, is a risk-reward proposition. Our inalienable right is the pursuit of happiness, not its attainment. Some who pursued happiness found that success and happiness are not the same thing. George Eastman was successful in business, giving away $100 million during his lifetime but ultimately took his own life. It is easy for us today to look back through the filter of history to this time and miss the bankruptcies, failures and heartbreak of other entrepreneurs working just down the street from Firestone or Wrigley.

From our viewpoint on the future side of these successes it is important not to forget that most of the innovators, famous or not, had no idea if their hours of hard work and experimentation would ever result in anything

14

worthwhile. Life in the early Twentieth Century was not lived inside a Norman Rockwell painting. For every one of today's household names made famous during this time there were hundreds or thousands more who labored in obscurity, never achieving success and frequently losing all they had only to try again out of necessity.

It is also easy for us to miss the men and women who innovated, worked and built successful businesses a century ago that will never be mentioned in history books, whose surnames have not come to stand for corporations, stock tickers, or automobile nameplates. Some of these stories are even more compelling than the well-known. Many of these entrepreneurs learned lessons and lived principles that are still very much applicable to us today.

Those of James Truslow Adams' generation saw the great innovations of Edison, Bell, and Ford, and the rapid progress and transition that came with them. They witnessed the marvelous transformation from gas light to electricity and from horse and buggy to automobile to airplane. They also saw great personal wealth amassed by a few powerful captains of industry who seemed to embody the optimism, and unfortunately greed, of the time. This generation experienced boom and bust, rapid expansion and depression. The American Dream, in the eyes of Adams was not success and wealth, not even the house with a white picket fence. Adams' dream was not about obtaining anything; rather Adams' dream was all about hard work and possibility.

2. Birth of an Entrepreneur

This was the America Ervin Phillip Arnold was born into on June 22, 1899, in rural Jackson County, Minnesota, the seventh of eight children. Ervin's parents, Anthony and Laura Arnold, were both born during the American Civil War. After their marriage, they moved west from their native Illinois and settled in western Iowa. Anthony tried farming for two years and then moved on to the small northwest Iowa town of Lake Park in 1884 where he built and operated the town's first hotel. In 1887, Anthony and Laura moved again, this time a few miles north of Lake Park, just across the Minnesota state line. Here, Anthony set out to break the sod of his new property in an attempt to carve out a farm and a life for his family. The Arnolds lived here for 16 years and it was on this farm that Ervin was born.

The three oldest Arnold children: George, Clyde, and Carl were all considerably older than Ervin. After these three came three girls: Loretta, Leona, and Pearl. The youngest of the family was Clayton, born four years after Ervin. There was nothing theoretical about the family's opportunity for work on a farm comprised of virgin prairie. The motivation for work was focused on day-to-day survival. Any long-term dream of wealth or success had to be relegated to the back of the mind. Nevertheless, the hard work on the Minnesota farm paid off greatly for the family, as the value of Anthony's land increased more than ten-fold during their years in Minnesota.

In 1901, the Federal Government opened up former Indian Reservation land in southwest Oklahoma for homesteaders. Anthony had been in one place for long enough, and he had seen first-hand the great success that can come from settling new land. In 1903, the family, with four-year-old Ervin and the younger Arnold children, packed up and headed to a farm Anthony purchased near Faxon, OK. The two oldest Arnold sons, George and Clyde had already moved out of the house. They stayed in Minnesota to pursue their own lives. Clayton, the youngest of the family was born during this time. The Faxon experiment lasted only a year and in 1904 the family returned to the Minnesota farm, the Oklahoma land proving far less prosperous than the Minnesota venture.

Before Ervin was old enough for high school, the family moved a few miles south, back across the Iowa border to an acreage near Lake Park. Less than a week after Ervin's fifteenth birthday, Archduke Franz Ferdinand, the heir to the throne of Austria-Hungary, was assassinated and the shadow of The Great War was cast across the world. The United States maintained neutrality throughout the beginning years of the war, but entered the conflict officially by declaring war on Germany two months before Ervin turned eighteen. Less than a year later, Ervin and the Lake Park class of 1918 graduated from high school. The class, comprised of six boys and nine girls, was the largest to graduate from the Lake Park school up to that time. On the day of their baccalaureate service, June 6, 1918, the United States Marine Corps suffered their largest number of single day casualties ever at the Battle of Belleau Wood. War was on the mind of everyone in the summer of 1918, especially an eighteen-year-old young man just graduating high school. There was no question if Ervin would participate in the war. The question was where and how.

Private Ervin Arnold

Shortly after graduation, Ervin was accepted to Iowa State University, then known as Iowa A & M, in Ames, where he enlisted in the Students Army Training Corps (SATC). According the War Department, the purpose of the SATC was to "utilize the executive and teaching personnel and the physical equipment of the educational institutions to assist in the training of our new armies. These facilities will be especially useful for the training of officer-candidates and technical experts of all kinds to meet the needs of the service." (The Students Army Training Corps, Second Edition, Descriptive Circular, 10/8/1918)

Retired Brigadier General James Rush Lincoln was on the faculty in Ames as a professor of military tactics and was initially put in charge of the SATC on campus. He administered the oath to induct 1,200 students, including Ervin, into the army in the fall of 1918. The corps was immediately put to the test with an outbreak of influenza on campus. At its height, there were 1,250 flu cases at one time. Within its first month, the SATC endured 51 flu-related deaths.

While in Ames, Private Arnold wrote this letter for publication in his hometown newspaper, the *Lake Park News*:

By the news I get from home you folks must be having quite a time with the Influenza. We are all over it here now and there was not many deaths, as just as soon as anyone begins feeling "punk" the military doctors make them go to bed and stay there until they are better. Our lieutenant told us that if anyone coughed or sneezed without putting his hand or a handkerchief over his mouth to knock him

19

down, and also if anyone spit on the floor or sidewalk to hit him hard. I like the drill fine but wish I was in some other camp where I did not have to study as we are not getting much out of school anyway.

Everyone here is just aching to be moved and to get to France as soon as possible, and I'm '"raring to go" since I have been in the army. Uncle Sam is mighty good to work for. We get good eats and have a dandy place to sleep. Of course we all get "bawled out" occasionally and if anyone can bawl you out it is a military officer. We have a "prince of a fellow" for our lieutenant. Leslie Horr, Irving Moe, and I are all in the same company but we are each in a different platoon. We got inoculated for typhoid last Saturday and para typhoid in the right arm, and inoculated in the left arm for small pox. They put 2,500,000 germs in us altogether but believe me our right arms felt like they had put in ten million. Here is a copy of orders someone composed down here.

General Orders of the Mess Hall

1. To take charge of the spuds and all gravy in view.

2. To watch my plate in a military manner, keeping always on the alert for any stray sausage that may come within sight, smell or hearing.

3. To report any bread sliced too thick to the mess sergeant.

4. To repeat all calls for meals.

5. To quit the table only when satisfied that nothing is left.

6. To receive but not pass on to the next man any meat, cabbage, or beans left by the non-coms, bucks, or cuckoos.

7. To talk to no one who asks for seconds

8. In case of fire in the mess hall to grab all eatables left by others in their escape.

9. To allow no one to steal anything in the line of grub.

10. To salute all chicken, beefsteak, pork chops, ham and eggs, and anything fit to eat

11. To be especially watchful at the table and during the time of eating, to challenge anyone who gets more prunes than myself.
Private Ervin Arnold S.A.T.C.I.S.C. Ames, IA

SATC members were considered to be "active duty. " They were on military payroll and lived under the same discipline and regulations as other soldiers. They were subject to military orders and could be transferred to other military facilities or overseas at any time. Some felt the SATC provided an easy way for college students to avoid combat and derisively referred to the program as "Safe At The College." Regardless of the intent or effectiveness of the program, armistice was signed on November 11, 1918, just a few months after the program's debut. Ervin Arnold was discharged from the Army and returned home the following month.

While Ervin was in the Army, his older brother Carl had started the Harris Lumber Company in 1917 in the nearby town of Harris, and built it into a successful business. Upon his return from the service, Ervin got a job working for Carl in the lumber yard, where he remained for about a year. In January of 1920, Ervin moved to Cherokee, Iowa to work for the Schoeneman Brothers Lumber Company. During visits home, he inspected the new automobile his father purchased in June. The purchase was noteworthy enough to appear in the local newspaper. The paper noted how much the family enjoyed the new automobile and surmised they would enjoy it even more, "as they become more used to running it." Such was the place of the automobile in rural Iowa life in 1920.

Ervin worked in Cherokee for two years, learning more about the lumber industry and expanding his business skills. In 1922, he was promoted to be the bookkeeper in the Schoeneman Brothers office in Spencer, Iowa, closer to his hometown of Lake Park. Moving closer to home also brought Ervin closer to Miss Irene Byers. After graduating from Lake Park High School in 1919, Irene attended Coe College in Cedar Rapids, Iowa. She then returned to Lake Park in the summer of 1921 to take a job as a teacher in a nearby country school, Silver Lake Number 2. Irene had been a year behind Ervin in school and had known him since childhood. In 1922, they were engaged to be married. Ervin saw another opportunity for advancement and accepted a job as manager of the Lane-Moore lumber yard in nearby Rembrandt, Iowa, moving there in July. On August 23, 1922 Ervin and Irene were married and made their first home in Rembrandt.

In addition to marriage, the summer of 1922 also saw Ervin make another change. After his wedding announcement, the name Ervin disappeared from all public record and Ervin Phillip was from then on known simply as E.P. Arnold. By the time of his death nearly sixty years later, only a very few of his many friends and acquaintances could tell you what E.P. really stood for. Employees had humorously decided it stood for Extra Profit.

E.P. displayed a definite knack for business, rising to the position of manager by the age of 23. This was due to his business instincts, his natural ability to relate well with people, and his skill and interest in the field of accounting. He had an outgoing, engaging personality and a keen intellect. He also had the advantage of a successful father and older brothers to help him get started in the business world. The fact that he was in the lumber business was immaterial. E.P. was simply good at business. E.P. decided to leave Rembrandt and the lumber yard industry after two years in his management position with Lane-Moore. It was time to pursue new opportunity.

In August of 1924, E.P. and Irene rented a house owned by Ralph Poole in nearby Spencer and E.P went to work as an accountant for the Dickson Fruit Company, a fruit wholesale warehouse. Ralph and his wife moved into the second floor apartment of his new downtown building and rented their home to the Arnolds. As had been the case with lumber, E.P. had no particular connection to the wholesale fruit business; it was merely a chance for growth. Spencer was the largest town within a hundred mile radius and offered more opportunity for E.P. to expand his own business aspirations. His move back to Spencer gave him exposure to many more possibilities. He soon was busy doing accounting and tax work after- hours for many entrepreneurs whose businesses were too small to warrant a full-time accountant.

E.P.'s father, Anthony Arnold had shown a willingness to move from industry to industry and from place to place in order to pursue the best life for himself and his family. By this time Anthony and Laura had lived near Sibley, Iowa; Lake Park, Iowa; Jackson, Minnesota; Faxon, Oklahoma;

back to Jackson, and finally back to Lake Park. E.P. showed this characteristic as well, and after leaving Rembrandt and the lumber industry for Spencer and wholesale fruit, E.P. saw another opportunity. In October of 1925, after a little over a year with Dickson, he accepted a position right next door to the Dickson warehouse at the Spencer Grocer Company warehouse, again working as an accountant.

At Spencer Grocer, E.P. honed his skills as an accountant and learned much about business in general from his new boss, R.M. Hicks. In 1961, E.P. told the Des Moines Register that Hicks, "taught me more about business than any man I ever worked for." During another interview in 1977, E.P. again credited Hicks for teaching him so much during his time working at Spencer Grocer Company saying, "The more I became involved with accounting the more I liked it. I didn't have a chance to go to college, but I learned through experience and the helpful coaching of my employers, especially R.M. Hicks." In addition to accounting, his early experiences in Spencer gave him good insight into wholesaling and management.

The entire time E.P. worked for Dickson and Spencer Grocer he continued to moonlight as an accountant. He also was formulating his own dream. By the time he went to work for R.M Hicks he already was mulling over a new business venture. Always on the lookout for opportunity, E.P. saw a great future for automobile parts and felt it could be a winning business. E.P. was also now married and had a good steady job, which made it more difficult to take a gamble on a venture of his own. In addition, he really didn't know anything about automobiles or automobile parts. In a 1959 interview, E.P. reflected on this time. "My boss was a sharp businessman and I learned a lot from him. From my association with the company, I felt that if wholesaling groceries and candy would pay, so would automotive parts wholesaling. Even so, I went right on keeping books. I was afraid to let go."

He had a vision of what he could do to take the next step in his career, but the next step was a big one. E.P. needed a spark, something to spur him to let go of his comfortable job and follow his instincts toward automotive parts wholesaling. Fortunately, that spark arrived in Spencer during October of 1926 in the form of Burr James Lewis.

3. B.J. Lewis

B.J. Lewis was five years older than E.P, born in southern Wisconsin on December 18, 1893. His family moved across the Mississippi River to the beautiful rolling landscape of rural Fayette County, Iowa where he was raised. After completing his schooling, B.J. worked a variety of odd jobs and spent some time in Des Moines studying electrical engineering. He traveled to South Dakota during harvest to work with oat threshing crews. He worked on road construction crews and briefly went into a garage business with Amos Babcock who would later become his brother-in-law.

On June 6, 1917, 23-year-old B.J. married school teacher Ruvie Babcock in nearby Waucoma, Iowa. Armed with a $50 wedding gift from his parents and money Ruvie had saved while teaching, the couple moved to a small house they bought in Des Moines. When registering for the draft, B.J. listed his occupation as mechanic. Only a few months into their marriage, B.J entered the service in World War I. According to B.J., "Upon discharge in 1919 jobs were hard to find because a depression then prevailed, and as a result I was unable to get steady employment for quite a spell."

In order to make ends meet, the young husband worked odd jobs in the area and was able to generate some income working as an agent for the B.F. Goodrich Company. His work for Goodrich put him in touch with the automotive industry where he would ultimately work for the rest of his career. The early years after the war were not easy for B.J. or many other soldiers who were returning to the Midwest from Europe.

Not only did he continue to struggle to find work, during this time he also fought health issues. In the fall of 1920, B.J. was admitted to the Mayo Clinic in Rochester, Minnesota for treatment of stomach ulcers. Treatment lasted for six months and used up nearly all of the money he had been able to set aside. By the time he was able to work again, the prospects for employment were still grim. B.J. was forced once again to take odd jobs and continue the search for full time employment. B.J. was not alone in his inability to find steady work. The entire state of Iowa was economically challenged as the agriculture-based society struggled to deal with the post-war reduction in demand for many of its products.

As the winter of 1921 arrived, B.J. and Ruvie decided that he had spent enough time looking for a job and decided to try a different path. They determined they would go into business for themselves instead. Given the rapidly increasing number of automobiles at the time, B.J. felt that an automobile machine shop would be a good business opportunity so they set out looking for a likely location. They left Des Moines and moved back closer to home, settling on New Hampton, Iowa, with a population of 2,500 as the site of their new venture. The small town of New Hampton was only 15 miles from where they had been wed four years earlier. As they prepared for this exciting new chapter in their lives, B.J. and Ruvie also discovered that Ruvie was pregnant. Since both came from close-knit families, the pregnancy made the decision to move closer to home that much easier.

With the money they made on the sale of the house in Des Moines plus money borrowed from a local bank, they opened up a small machine shop in a rented New Hampton building in the spring of 1922. A few months later, on October 22, Ruvie gave birth to their son James. Needing a more accommodating location for his shop work, B.J. borrowed more money and built a building in New Hampton specifically for the shop in 1923. For the next three years, B.J. worked diligently in the machine shop, constantly looking for ways to increase its profitability. Finally in 1926 B.J. decided that an automotive machine shop business was not sustainable in New Hampton. With a wife and young son to care for, he had to try something else. He was forced to accept that his effort of the last three years was, in his words, "a failure as a business."

By the time B.J. decided his machine shop business could not survive, he was 32 years old. He had been married for nine years and had a four year old son. He had fought in a war, battled stomach ulcers, been turned down for jobs at every turn, and failed in business. B.J was definitely not living the American Dream in the fall of 1926. Fortunately for his family and for all the people who would eventually work for the companies he started, he did have two components of the American Dream operating in his life: hard work and perseverance.

The New Hampton venture was not a complete failure, as B.J. did make enough profit on the sale of the building to attempt a new enterprise. He still felt the automobile industry held potential but could neither justify nor afford investing in another capital- intensive machine shop operation. He decided on selling automobile parts and accessories. Now, once again he needed a location. By the time B.J. and Ruvie celebrated young James' fourth birthday, they had picked a town with a larger population than New Hampton but without the significant automotive parts competition that was already found in the larger cities.

Armed with the small profit from the sale of their building, B.J. and Ruvie packed up their meager belongings and moved to the opposite side of the state, settling in Spencer, a northwest Iowa town of 5,000 people. On October 20, 1926, the local Spencer newspaper notified its subscribers that a new business was about to be established in town: "B.J. Lewis from New Hampton is opening an automobile accessory agency in the Wertz building on 4th and Mill Streets. He will move to Spencer about the first of November." No doubt E.P. Arnold read this particular notice with some interest.

4. Spencer, Iowa

Iowa achieved statehood in 1846. At that time the population of the state was nearly 100,000. Early population had centered in areas of timber since wood was required for buildings, fences, and fuel. As a result, the mostly flat unbroken prairie around Spencer was among the last places in the state to be settled. The first settlement in all of Clay County did not occur until 1855. When the Civil War ended ten years later, the area that was ultimately to become Spencer was still completely uninhabited.

Over a million soldiers were exiting the service after the war in 1865. There was much concern for their integration back into civilian society. Most had no jobs to return to and life had changed significantly since they had left. The unsettled areas in Iowa became a common destination for Civil War veterans looking for a place to create a new life.

Spencer Grove was a small wooded area at the confluence of two small rivers in the middle of Clay County. The grove was named for George E. Spencer, a United States Senator from Alabama who had spent some time living in the state of Iowa. It was here that a small group of veterans came in the fall of 1865 to establish homesteads.

By the time a plat was surveyed for a town six years later, there was already a core group of established stores and residences. Immigration to Clay County tended to be to the north side of the county and residents felt the current county seat of Peterson in the southwest corner was too far away for county business. Spencer was at the center of Clay County and seemed a more desirable location for the seat of county government. In 1871, Clay County residents voted to move the county seat to Spencer by a count of 359 to 200. Spencer's fortunate location and newfound status as county seat quickly brought business and growth to the town and the demand for the newly platted lots increased rapidly.

In 1885, 20-year-old Harry Heikens came to Clay County with his brother Richard to work a farm their father had purchased north of Spencer. They bought two plows and set to work breaking through the hard sod to expose the rich black Iowa soil. It was a slow, labor intensive project. The hardness of the sod necessitated that they stop each time around the field, remove the blade from the plow and hammer it back into shape for another round. Eventually the brothers and their plows prevailed and turned the prairie land into a fertile farm.

Spencer Main Street in the early 1910's

In 1911, Harry bought one of the first automobiles in the area, a Maxwell. He was so impressed with the car that a few years later he moved to Spencer and started one of the first automobile dealerships in town. There, he sold and repaired Maxwell automobiles with his son George. They continued this business until Harry retired in 1926.

By the 1920s, the fifty-year-old town of Spencer had grown to a progressive business hub, and the largest town in the region. Many of the established businesses in town were owned by second- or third- generation descendants of the town fathers. Each year, there were many Civil War veterans still marching in the Armistice Day parade. Anyone who wanted to know what it was like to live in a sod house or deal with the threat of an Indian raid only needed to ask one of the older residents. Automobiles were becoming more common but there was still no paved road leading to town.

The 1920s saw an explosion of automobile use across the state, and Spencer was no exception. Dealers of different brands of cars were springing up all over town. Within an eight block stretch of Spencer's main street were:

Holmes Motor Company selling Fords

Fred Moore's Overland and Willys-Knight dealership

Ralph Poole's Case Cars dealership

Asher Motor Company selling Dodge

Lowe and Erickson Company selling Essex, Hudson and Packard

H & N Chevrolet and Buick

Early car dealers in the area sold their wares to a quickly growing market despite repressed economic conditions. The number of automobiles registered in Iowa doubled between 1922 and 1927 to 711,951 vehicles. During this time, most people were purchasing an automobile for the first time. It was not uncommon for dealers to send a representative home with the new automobile owners to spend a couple of days training them on the use of their new vehicle.

Spencer Auto Supply was an automotive parts wholesaling business established in Spencer. The company had been in existence for several years under several different owners. In October, 1925, it was sold to Charles Curtis and his father-in-law O.C. Reiste, who renamed it R and C Auto Supply Co.

In May, 1921 fifty-year-old R.M. Hicks of New Ulm, Minnesota liked what he saw in Spencer, Iowa. Already a successful businessman, R.M. sold his grocery warehouse business in New Ulm and moved to Spencer to start a similar company. Four and a half years later, he hired E.P. Arnold as an accountant. Mr. Hicks was well connected with area businessmen. In the fall of 1926, he received a tip from a colleague in New Ulm that the three banks in Spencer were all in a precarious financial position. The grocer company had money in all three banks and Mr. Hicks withdrew all of his deposits, allowing him to have access to cash the next week when all three banks closed their doors.

5. Not so Roaring '20s

Electricity, motion pictures, telephones and automobiles were all invented prior to the 1920s but that decade was the first to see widespread popular availability of these modern amenities. Life after the First World War was certainly different than before, partially due to these innovations. Much of the glamor, prosperity and economic growth often associated with the decade known as the Roaring '20s was not experienced by the typical resident of the Midwest. In his *A History of Iowa*, Leland Sage points out what he calls the great paradox of the 1920s: "urban prosperity side by side with rural depression."

Much of the reason for the economic trouble in Iowa and the surrounding states during this decade was due to the struggling agricultural economy in the wake of the war. During World War I, the rallying cry coming from Washington DC and local bankers was "Food will win the war!" Government officials encouraged bankers to loan farmers the money they needed to turn pastures and meadows into tilled farmland in order to increase production. Farmers were encouraged to till closer to property lines and maximize tillable ground. Guaranteed minimum prices were put in effect by the federal government for many agricultural products .This created a local economy based on the doubly dangerous condition of artificially high prices on artificially high production.

Fueled by the unsustainable profits during the war years, some farmers overextended themselves with debt. The agriculture industry developed the means to produce more than the non-wartime economy could absorb after the hostilities ended. In order to ease the transition back to an open market economy, price guarantees continued to be enforced on many agricultural products through 1919. When price supports were removed, farmers found the prices they received for their produce dropped dramatically, while costs of the items they purchased continued to rise. This profound reduction in purchasing power was a painful lesson to many farmers who found bankruptcy the only solution to paying the debt they had incurred to expand their production. Prior to World War I, approximately 5.5% of bankruptcies nationwide involved a farmer. In 1920, that number nearly tripled, sending shock waves through the agriculture community and banks in rural Iowa.

As farmers were declaring bankruptcy and watching their purchasing power wither, banks were reeling from the reduction in value of their collateral holdings, which often left them unable to cover deposits. While suspension of business in a bank only happened 58 times in 1910, eight of the ten years in the 1920s saw over 500 such suspensions. Of course, a failed bank meant loss of assets, or at least interrupted cash flow, for a wide variety of non-agricultural businesses and individuals. Farmers with less purchasing power spent less money in small town businesses. The ripples of the post-war farm crisis affected everyone in agriculturally-based Iowa.

Despite the gloomy economic conditions in the state, Iowa was actually among the leaders in the use of automobiles. The nature of the state, with many small towns at reasonable distances from each other, and the lack of railroad coverage in many places put a premium on the use of automobiles as they became more affordable. In fact, by the late 1920s, Iowa had more automobiles per capita than any other state in the union.

With the explosion of automobile use, the federal government had been discussing a federal highway program for several years. In 1925, construction of federal highways began in earnest. One of the first US highways became the most famous. Route 66 stretched from Chicago to Los Angeles. Towns and businesses along Route 66 formed the US Highway 66 Association which lobbied law-makers and advertised to encourage the motoring public to use the new highway. During the 1920s, the attention generated by the US Highway 66 Association started many similar enterprises centering around other highways across the country. Highway 66 was the first to be completely paved when its paving was finished in 1938.

Because of the high cost of paving roads and the difficult economic times, there was considerable resistance to paving in 1920s Iowa. In 1924, F.R. White, the Chief Engineer of the Iowa State Highway Commission addressed this issue at the Iowa Automobile Merchants Association convention when he said, "Some people seem to be constitutionally opposed to hard surfaced roads. Their opposition at times has the strength of religious fanaticism. As a matter of fact, there is no justification for anyone to take the position of being blindly opposed to paving or blindly in favor of such improvements...Motor vehicles can be operated over pavement more cheaply than over a dirt or graveled road....The Iowa dirt roads are perhaps among the finest dirt roads in the country when they are sufficiently dry to be firm and stable and sufficiently wet not to be dusty. This happy condition, however, seldom prevails."

B.J. Lewis was not moving to an economic boom town when he came to Spencer in the fall of 1926, but he was no stranger to hardship and hard work. He was armed with strong knowledge of the automotive industry, experience in a machine shop, tenacity, and some cash from the sale of his New Hampton building. He found a small storefront to rent, a block east of Main Street. There, he opened his automobile parts and accessories store. He rented a house for the family a short four block walk to the south of the store. B.J. had plenty of industry experience and all the characteristics he hoped were necessary to run a successful auto parts store. The one thing he lacked was training and experience in accounting, which proved to be a liability as he entered into his new venture.

Spencer, Iowa Main Street in the early 1920's

6. Partnership

As B.J. Lewis opened his doors for business late in 1926, he knew he would need help with bookkeeping. B.J. and E.P. Arnold met at a card game and quickly became friends. Learning of E.P.'s bookkeeping background, B.J. extended an invitation for his new friend to come visit his store and take a look at his operation. B.J. had started out using cigar boxes to store receipts and invoices. As E.P. began to inspect the documents and help B.J. formulate his accounting books, it quickly became apparent to him that the margin to be made on automobile parts was much higher than on grocery items. Harry Heikens had just retired and closed his automobile dealership and parts store and the time seemed right to take the leap into business that he had been considering.

E.P. and B.J. realized that they both provided value to each other. B.J. brought an understanding of the automobile industry, machine shop expertise, and three years of experience running his own business. E.P. had strong accounting skills, excellent business acumen, and an understanding of extending credit and wholesaling. E.P. was also very well known in Spencer and the surrounding area. They had very different but complementing personalities. E.P. was more friendly and outgoing, while B.J. was more introverted and serious. Despite the differences, the two got along well with each other. E.P. and Irene even moved and rented a house across the street from B.J., Ruvie, and James. In less than a year after B.J.'s arrival in Spencer, the two were ready to begin the venture that would drastically change both of their lives.

The partners made the decision to combine an automotive parts store with a machine shop to make a single entity that was more diversified than either would have been alone. The partners each invested $500. E.P. used his entire savings of $300 and borrowed $200 from a friend. Their shared investment let them buy some machine shop equipment, their first inventory of parts to sell, and the first month's rent. Initially, Arnold would focus on selling parts and doing the book work and Lewis on running the machine shop. The building Lewis had rented on East 4th Street was not large enough to accommodate their plans so they sought a more desirable location to rent.

Most of the automotive businesses in Spencer at the time were clustered on the north end of Main Street. In the middle of this section was the Peter Ostrom building. Mr. Ostrom had come to the area as a young boy in 1871 when he and his family emigrated from Sweden. Peter had farmed and then moved into town where he started a feed business which he ran until his retirement. Upon retiring, he closed his business, moved back to his farm, and rented out his building.

When B.J. moved to Spencer in 1926, the Ostrom Building was occupied by the Olson Brothers clothing store which closed its doors during the spring of 1927. Arnold and

Lewis quickly identified the building as a perfect location for their new enterprise but determined it was still not big enough to house the machine shop they planned to operate. Peter Ostrom agreed to build a cement block addition to the back of the building to house the machine shop. According to the local newspaper, the cement addition would "house the tools and machinery to be used in finishing pistons and other parts." Ostrom also approved some remodeling in the front of the store to fit the parts business they envisioned.

On August 10, 1927 with preparations for the building nearly complete, the partnership of Arnold and Lewis opened its doors. On the same day, President Calvin Coolidge was in South Dakota at the dedication ceremony to commence blasting at Mount Rushmore. Babe Ruth was two thirds of the way to his record setting 60 home runs. That weekend the federal government would announce a budget surplus of over $2 billion for the fiscal year.

Arnold and Lewis now faced two major hurdles in their effort to get the automotive parts portion of their business off the ground. First, they had to differentiate themselves from existing competition. Second, they had to convince large manufacturers to sell them merchandise COD since they had no cash flow to buy inventory and could not establish credit.

From the beginning of the company, E.P. Arnold was adamant that they would not attempt to beat their competitors on price. He believed their customers would gladly pay them a higher price as long as they could

42

provide clearly superior service. They also made the decision to focus exclusively on selling to garages and not spend too much effort on advertising to the general public. Since garages did not get paid for their repairs until the work was done, it stood to reason they would buy from the jobber who could supply the needed parts the quickest. E.P. commented on this strategy a few years later saying, "The idea appealed to us that if a better means could be found to speed delivery of parts and accessories at a reasonable cost to dealers that an automotive jobbing business was assured."

The *Spencer Reporter* article describing their beginning calls attention to the innovation that may have been more responsible for the early success of Arnold and Lewis than any other, noting that "a specially equipped delivery car will cover the adjacent territory on regular schedule, making deliveries to garages and car dealers." It was this delivery concept that would set Arnold and Lewis apart.

The first attempt to meet the need for speedy delivery was a 1927 Chevrolet Roadster that the partners modified with a wooden storage box in the back to carry parts. Arnold and Lewis met with some local mechanics to find the parts they most commonly needed. Armed with this knowledge, E.P. would purchase these parts COD and carry them with him on his sales route through the territory. This method proved successful immediately and allowed the new business to begin making sales and establish relationships with the mechanics in the area.

The growing partnership soon bought out their primary competition in Spencer, the R and C Auto Supply Company. As they continued to expand, it became apparent that someone with automotive experience would be more effective in the sales position than E.P.. In 1928, they hired Arlo Everett, who had been the parts manager for the Chevrolet Dealer in town. Everett took over the traveling sales route, which allowed E.P. time to work at the counter inside the store and handle the growing book work. Arnold was also able to spend more time working with manufacturers to secure sales rights for a growing list of lines, allowing them to meet more needs of their customer base.

The rapidly growing business was not the only excitement for the partners in 1928. Irene Arnold was pregnant with the couple's first child. On January 24, 1929, Irene gave birth to a son. Stewart Byron was born in the couple's modest bungalow on East Park Street. It was a joyous occasion for the Arnolds as well as both sets of grandparents who traveled down from Lake Park to visit their most recent grandchild. Unfortunately, the joy over Stewart's birth was to be short lived. Only a few months later he became very ill with flu-like symptoms. By the time doctors were able to diagnose the cause as spinal meningitis, it was too late. After eight days of illness Stewart passed away on March 5, victim to a disease with an extremely high infant mortality rate in the 1920s. Stewart's death took place one day after Herbert Hoover was sworn in as the 31st President of The United States.

As E.P. and Irene dealt with the loss of their son, they were also working through changes with the partnership. E.P. and B.J. had been working with lawyers to incorporate the company. In the short time since the beginning of the partnership, their initial $500 investments had already grown to $1,418 each and the company listed assets of nearly $14,000. On May 8, 1929, stock certificates were issued for Arnold and Lewis Incorporated. The articles of incorporation listed B.J. Lewis as President and E.P. Arnold as Board Secretary. The Board of directors consisted of B.J., E.P. and Irene.

By the second anniversary of Arnold and Lewis, the company had grown into a very successful operation. E.P. and Irene decided to take a much-needed vacation after a difficult several months. They set out westward to travel through the South Dakota badlands, and then headed to Denver Colorado where they would take in the scenery of the Rocky Mountains. They traveled for two weeks and then returned to Spencer where E.P. was anxious to get back to work.

The partners were poised to hire additional bookkeeping help and began to talk of expansion. In the fall of 1929, E.P. contacted the Spencer High School and asked for recommendations for recent graduates who had typing and bookkeeping skills. The school recommended three young ladies who had exhibited skill in these areas and E.P. interviewed all three. One of the three was Florence Pullen who had been successful in high school typing competitions and had begun taking accounting classes following her graduation. E.P. offered the bookkeeping job to Florence and she readily accepted.

When she reminded E.P. of her minimal accounting training, E.P. wasn't concerned. He told her he would teach her everything she needed to know, saying he preferred she learn his way of doing things anyway. Florence promptly dropped her accounting classes and set out to learn on the job. There was no office space in the small store and they didn't have a desk, so E.P. and B.J. moved a small table between two file cabinets along the side wall of the store. Along with a small safe, this area made up the workspace for their new employee.

There was much discussion around town regarding how the paving of U.S. Highway 71 would affect business. Spencer sat at the intersection of U.S. Highway 71 running north to south and U.S. Highway 18 running east to west. Through 1929, both of these highways were still gravel and could be difficult to travel on during bad weather. Plans were in the works to pave Highway 71 north of Spencer to the county line the following summer and this news generated some excitement within the business community.

Through the winter, the store was able to carry more lines and deliver to more customers, and business continued to grow. The customer relationships developed through their rapid deliveries attracted machine shop business, which generated more business for replacement parts. The partners had a winning business formula and began to discuss the idea of replicating the operation in other locations. B.J. and Ruvie were excited to finally have a successful business venture, but at the same time were homesick for their families in the eastern part of the state. B.J. would later write, "we were not exactly pleased with the Spencer locality and desired to live in Eastern Iowa, nearer our people and original homes." B.J. set out to find a location nearer his eastern Iowa roots to establish another store.

As summer approached, B.J. found a nearly bankrupt auto parts business in Waterloo, Iowa called All-States Parts Service and began negotiations with the owners and their major creditors. In May, E.P. and Irene embarked on a two week trip east where they stopped in Detroit to visit Henry Ford's main manufacturing plant. They crossed into Canada and came down to Niagara Falls and then continued through New York to Pennsylvania, where they heard President Hoover give his Decoration Day address from Gettysburg. From there, the Arnolds traveled to Washington DC, visited Arlington National Cemetery, and Mount Vernon. They drove home through Ohio and Indiana. Upon their return E.P. remarked how much he enjoyed the trip and that he preferred the sites on this eastern trip over their trip west a year earlier.

By July, B.J. had reached an agreement to take over management of All-States Parts Service and the partners made arrangements for him to move east to run this store. In August, 1930, B.J., Ruvie, and seven-year-old James packed up their belongings and moved to Waterloo, where B.J. assumed management of the store there. E.P. continued to manage the Spencer store with the help of

Florence Pullen who had been with him long enough to handle much of the bookkeeping duties.

B.J. was able to turn around the Waterloo business, growing it quickly into a profitable enterprise. He took ownership of All-States Parts Service and re-named it Lewis Motor Supply. Arlo Everett, the former Chevrolet Parts Manager who was employed by Arnold and Lewis, agreed to move to Waterloo to work for B.J. Lewis Motor Supply went on to become a very successful Waterloo business that would continue on for over fifty years, through three generations of the Lewis family.

E.P. Arnold was also looking at expansion and was bolstered by the success his partner was having in Waterloo. While he was a freelance accountant in Spencer, E.P. had a conversation with an IRS Agent during an audit of one of his clients. The auditor had recently come from Marshall, Minnesota and remarked that a good environment for business existed in that city. That conversation planted a seed in E.P.'s mind, and when he set out to open a new location, he settled on Marshall as the site for the new branch.

Marshall was the county seat of Lyon County, Minnesota, a town of 3,200 people located 120 miles north and west of Spencer. Just as Lewis had assumed ownership of Lewis Motor Supply separately from the Arnold and Lewis Corporation, E.P. opened the branch in Marshall as Arnold Motor Supply. He offered Irene's 22-year-old brother, Paul Byers, the opportunity to manage the new branch and allowed Paul to invest in the enterprise as a partner. E.P.

purchased two delivery trucks for the Marshall store and hired two salesmen drivers.

With both Arnold and Lewis confident that their individual ventures were on sound footing, they decided that E.P. would buy out B.J.'s share of the Arnold and Lewis Corporation and operate the Spencer and Marshall locations as Arnold Motor Supply. Meanwhile, B.J. would continue in Waterloo, focusing on growing Lewis Motor Supply. In June, E.P. Arnold bought all of Lewis' shares, and the partners wrote up the papers to dissolve the Arnold and Lewis Corporation. The dissolution notice was signed by all parties on Friday, June 26, 1931.

E.P. Arnold behind the counter of the first store

7. Fire!

The next day, Saturday, June 27, dawned hot and windy. The strong southwest wind brought no relief from the stifling heat. It had been a busy time for Florence Pullen who had now been employed by E.P. Arnold for eighteen months. She was glad she decided to take the job with Mr. Arnold rather than pursue her original plan to take accounting classes. She believed she had probably learned more from him than she would have from the classes, and she was getting paid to do it. In addition to her learning, there was a lot going on at work, with Mr. Lewis moving on to Waterloo and the new Arnold Motor Supply store in Minnesota. This Saturday the town was abuzz with plans for the upcoming Fourth of July festivities. Many stores had patriotic displays in the front windows. There was a lot to talk about, but that day, as the temperature eclipsed the 100 degree mark, most were simply talking about the weather.

As she liked to do on Saturdays, Florence met some friends for lunch. After lunch they visited a few stores to do some shopping. They had parked in front of the Clay County Bank, not far from the Arnold and Lewis store. As they were nearing completion of their shopping excursion they heard what they assumed to be gunfire, followed by an explosion that shook the ground. Frightened, they quickly headed out to the car, thinking they should leave the area. Once out on the sidewalk they were joined by what seemed to be hundreds of people who were streaming out of the Main Street businesses. A few of them were armed, thinking perhaps the bank was being robbed. Upon reaching the street, they were amazed to find rockets, fireworks and flames shooting out of the front windows of the Otto A. Bjornstad Drug Store on the corner of 4th and Main.

What the shoppers had assumed to be gunfire was actually an open flame that had been accidentally dropped into a fireworks display, igniting the highly flammable and explosive contents. Exactly who dropped what into the display has been lost to history, but the results were catastrophic. Above the burning drugstore, Northwestern Bell telephone operators were frantically issuing calls for help, knowing that once the fire spread upstairs to the exchange, there would be no telephone service anywhere in the town.

As soon as the fire department arrived on the scene, ladders were used to rescue the operators who had remained at their post to help communicate with authorities in other area towns. By the time they climbed out the window, smoke was thick and the heat was rapidly growing in intensity. Florence and her friends quickly moved north, away from the fire, and watched from across the street of Arnold and Lewis as the firemen attempted to contain the growing inferno.

51

As they watched in horror, a second major explosion rocked the drug store, sending flames and debris airborne. The strong winds carried them across the street, setting fire to awnings in front of two stores. Another rocket shot across the street, igniting another awning, which the powerful wind soon blew up and through an open second story window. Patrons watching a Saturday matinee up the street had been oblivious to the commotion outside, but as the fire crossed the street, the smell of smoke soon permeated the theater.

It was quickly becoming obvious that the fire department had neither the equipment nor adequate water pressure to fight the inferno on its own. Even the asphalt street in front of Bjornstad's drug store was melting and starting to burn while the fire continued to spread up the street, propelled by the powerful south wind.

Fourteen miles to the north, the Milford fire alarm had started to ring around twenty minutes after the start of the blaze. Aided by the newly paved stretch of Highway 71 between Spencer and Milford, the Milford crew was the first out-of-town fire department on the scene. As the wind continued to blow the flames north and east, concern was growing for two particularly vulnerable facilities: Schoneman Brothers Lumber and Lewis Vander Hoff's gas station. Firefighters knew that if either of these buildings were allowed to catch fire, their highly flammable contents could cause catastrophic problems.

With the telephone exchange destroyed, no phone calls could be placed from within Spencer, so residents set off driving to nearby towns to call for help. A telegraph operator working from the bank across the street to the south of Bjornstad's drug store was safe from the flames that were being blown to the north. However, the extreme heat forced her to stop her feverish work communicating with the outside world while she relocated farther from the fire. Soon, the Ruthven and Spirit Lake fire departments were en-route to battle the spreading disaster.

Fire crews from over 30 miles away could see the billowing smoke from the fire as they raced to Spencer's aid. Those coming from towns to the south were ironically hampered by the road paving work which had Highway 71 closed, sending them on a lengthy detour. Residents north and east of downtown raced from place to place fighting flames, as embers and burning debris blew onto rooftops causing flame-ups across the neighborhood. With all of the available firefighters occupied fighting the main fire downtown, residents knew any fire that caught hold in the residential district would be unstoppable.

Florence Pullen and hundreds of other spectators were powerless to do anything to aid in the fight. There was already a shortage of water pressure and fire equipment, so most could only stand by helplessly and watch. At 5:00 an urgent telegram was sent to the Des Moines Register, asking them to send their airplane to Spencer loaded with dynamite so a building could be demolished as a firebreak. George Yates, the Register aerial photographer and pilot, took off in the company plane along with the Des Moines fire chief, explosives experts, other firefighting experts and a load of dynamite. Aided by the same southerly wind that was threatening to spread fire across the town, the plane made it to Spencer in a record sixty minutes.

On the ground, exhausted firefighters continued to do everything they could to stop the flames' advance. On the west side of the street where the fire had started they were winning the battle, but the fire was still marching north unchecked up the east side of the street toward the Peter Ostrom building. Next door to the south of the Ostrom building was Spencer Drycleaning. The proprietors there had started removing all of the contents of the building as soon as they saw the fire start to spread, so by the time the dynamite arrived, all of the clothing had been removed. E.P. used this time to remove all of his bookkeeping records from the store, but did not have enough time to salvage the inventory.

The decision was made to blast the dry cleaner's building to create a gap between buildings. This would hopefully allow the firefighters to halt the advancing flames which had been spreading from building to building. With the dynamite delivered, the charge was set and soon the two story building had collapsed upon itself from the blast. Fire continued to burn into the Peter Ostrom building, destroying E.P. Arnold's entire inventory and machine shop equipment. The solid wall between the Ostrom Building and the Hurd Building to the north held. Arnold and Lewis was the last business lost in the fire. Losses for E.P. were listed at $13,500. E.P. was devastated. He had some insurance, but not nearly enough to cover the loss.

From across the street and a safe distance up from the blast, Florence watched the devastation. She wondered what would happen to the job she had grown to enjoy and feared for the safety and well-being of her friends and neighbors. By 7:30 that evening, approximately four hours from the initial blast in the drugstore, the fire was subdued enough to be deemed under control. Chemicals in the basement of Bjornstad Drug still smoldered and burned, but for the most part, the fire was out.

An estimated 10,000 people milled about Spencer Saturday night. Many were in shock as they surveyed the damage which spread nearly three full blocks up Main Street, encompassing seventy five businesses and numerous personal apartments. Estimates indicated as many as 500 people like Florence watched their workplace go up in flames. The next day, people from hundreds of miles in every direction descended on Spencer to see the devastation for themselves. The Sunday Des Moines Register carried stunning pictures of the remains of downtown Spencer and word of the fire spread across the country.

Local resident Chris Johnson was returning home from a visit to his native Denmark. In New York, when he attempted to purchase a train ticket back to Spencer, the ticket agent told him not to go to Spencer because he wasn't sure if there was anything left to return to. Spencer Mayor W.H. Lewis issued a statement for the Sunday Des Moines Register, "Although this was a terrible cost to the community, the people of this town are not discouraged. We will rebuild bigger and better."

55

E.P. Arnold wasted no time making plans to get back into business. His good friend Theron Lowe owned Lowe and Erickson Company, the Hudson and Packard dealership and service station located a block north of the Peter Ostrom Building. First thing Monday morning, Theron made room for E.P. and Florence to set up a table in the corner of his showroom so they could take orders, pay bills, process receivables and get the business back on its feet. That night, the City Council met in special session to issue regulations and permits for temporary structures which would allow businesses to continue functioning during the rebuilding process. During the stay in the Lowe building, E.P. was particularly interested in the automotive painting operation and spoke frequently with Earl McCleary, who ran that portion of the business.

The city of Spencer now found itself at a crossroads. With a good portion of the downtown business district lying in ruin, the lack of facilities could have bankrupted some Spencer businesses. It was imperative that rebuilding begin at once to encourage business owners to reinvest in the town. Work on cleaning up the debris began almost immediately and a central office was set up to facilitate insurance adjusters with the process of paying insurance claims. Temporary wood and tin structures popped up along Main Street and business owners started placing orders to replace their burned inventories.

Within a month, the rubble clearing was essentially done and plans had been drawn up to start construction on the new buildings. On July 23, the Spencer News Herald published drawings and descriptions of many of the buildings that would be going up, among them was the new Peter Ostrom building. E.P. and Florence continued to work out of a corner of the Lowe Motor Company building while closely following the progress of the construction. Spencer was a whirlwind of cleanup, construction, and moving for the next several months. The story of the recovery caught the eye of President Hoover who sent a telegram to the Spencer Reporter, "I am interested to learn of the courage and enterprise with which the businessmen of Spencer, Iowa, have restored the portion of the city destroyed with such heavy loss last June, and extend to the community my hearty congratulations on its spirit and achievement."

Finally, nearly three months after the fire, Arnold Motor Supply was able to move back into the newly completed Ostrom Building on September 24. The News Herald noted, "The entire stock is not as yet in place, but the new all-steel cases and rack are being rapidly filled and Mr. Arnold expects to be operating normally within the week." Thanks to the coming- together of business and civic leaders for the common good, Spencer quickly emerged from the disaster with a beautiful new downtown area that exhibited a shared architecture in the Art Deco style. Thanks to sales from the branch location in Marshall, Minnesota, the generosity of Mr. Arnold's friend Theron Lowe, and Peter Ostrom's quick rebuilding, Arnold Motor Supply was able to thrive during and after an event that could have ended the business before it really had a chance to bloom.

Though it wasn't an official government holiday in 1931, there was a tradition dating back to Abraham Lincoln for each President to declare a day of Thanksgiving every fall. In 1931, President Herbert Hoover declared November 26, "as a National Day of Thanksgiving, and do recommend that our people rest from their daily labors and in their homes and accustomed places of worship give devout thanks for the blessings which a merciful Father has bestowed upon us." People across Spencer had much to be thankful for. The town had emerged from the devastation of the fire, and life was slowly returning to normal. E.P. and Irene also had reason to be thankful. By the end of 1931, the company had grown to have in excess of $32,000 in assets and E.P. now had over $21,000 invested. They were moving to a slightly larger rental house on East 3rd Street, and Irene was once again pregnant. The following summer, on July 27, 1932, she gave birth to another son, Merrill.

The Arnold and Lewis store during the Spencer Fire of 1931

8. Branching Out

With Paul Byers in Marshall, E.P. needed more help in both stores and hired Kieth Byers, another of Irene's brothers, to work in Spencer. He hired a young Spencer High School graduate named Thomas Kemis to work for Paul in Marshall. When E.P. needed some help cleaning up the store and shop area, he asked Florence if she knew anyone who could come in and help out. She immediately thought of her boyfriend, LeRoy Rusch who was working as a farmhand for area farmers. LeRoy started out cleaning and doing odd jobs for the company, glad to be working for Mr. Arnold and glad to be working closer to Florence.

E.P. Arnold had borrowed money to establish his branch location in Marshall, Minnesota and his investment was proving fruitful. As the Spencer and Marshall locations grew in profitability, E.P. decided he should add another store to continue the growth of his young company. Bankers who held his loans for the Marshall branch were less optimistic. The country was in the midst of the Great Depression and conventional wisdom held that E.P. should use his profits to retire his existing debt.

E.P. knew his business and understood the market for automotive parts in the area. He was confident that a branch established in nearby Sheldon, Iowa would be as profitable as Marshall had been. Sheldon was a town similar to Spencer, though slightly smaller. Started in 1872, it had a population of 3,320 in 1930 and was located 35 miles to the west of Spencer. As 1932 drew to a close, E.P. had secured financing and agreed to lease space for the new store in the Security National Investment Company building on 9th Street.

In looking for a manager for this location, he remembered the time he had spent with Earl McCleary, who handled the automotive paint for Lowe and Erickson. He felt Earl would make an excellent store manager. Earl agreed to take on the challenge and on December 15, 1932, Arnold Motor Supply number three opened in Sheldon, Iowa. As a testament to the difficult economic conditions of the time, one of the local Sheldon banks was declared insolvent the next day. Three months later, the nation inaugurated Franklin D. Roosevelt as its thirty-second president.

Five years later, E.P. would look back at the decision to expand into Sheldon and remark, "We recall distinctly the advice and warnings of friends who urged against our decision to establish any new branches at that time. The nation was on the brink of the greatest financial and commercial upheaval in its history. Weighed against their advice and warnings was one single factor that was to determine our course - our belief and faith in the community and its citizens. We were not mistaken, for this store, thanks to your loyalty and friendship, has proven a sound step."

In February, 1933, J.C. Penney made a personal visit to Spencer. He presided over a meeting of the managers and staff of J.C. Penney stores in the area. While in town, he also met with local business leaders, including E.P. Arnold, to discuss his own business philosophy. Mr. Penney frequently encouraged his store managers to buy into their store as a part owner. He also felt it was important to share profits with store managers to give them a stake in the company's success. The business tenets shared by J.C. Penney resonated with E.P. Arnold and solidified his own developing philosophy.

With three stores to run, E.P. decided it was time to hire a full time Sales Manager to oversee sales across the entire organization. Thus far, E.P. had hired known entities for every significant position in his company after his first hire of Florence Pullen. For the Sales Manager position, E.P. went completely outside the area and brought in L.A. Forbord, a sales executive from Canton, Ohio, who was working for Berger Manufacturing Company, a manufacturer of steel office and retail fixtures. Mr. Forbord joined the company in April, 1934 and lasted only six months. This experience was an anomaly in E.P.'s track record of hiring leaders who would stay with the company for many years, often the remainder of their careers.

After the addition of the Sheldon store, E.P. continued to plan for expansion. His brother-in-law Paul had invested with him has a partner in the Marshall store. Encouraged by his conversation with J.C. Penney, E.P. decided that managers would always have a financial stake in the company. In addition to Paul and Kieth, a third Byers brother, Robert, was joining the company to work in the Spencer store. Paul was still in Marshall, Kieth moved to Sheldon to manage the store there, and Robert was put in charge of the Spencer store. LeRoy Rusch was sent to Sheldon to work as a salesman for Kieth. E.P. invited both Kieth and Robert to invest, and reorganized the company as a corporation. On April 1, 1935, Arnold Motor Supply Inc. was organized with E.P. as President. Irene and Kieth joined E.P. on the board of directors. Paul was listed as Vice President and Robert as Secretary.

The corporation was poised to expand again. The addition of new customers to the east of Spencer made it desirable to expand eastward. After looking for a likely location, the town of Algona was chosen to be home to the fourth store. Algona, county seat of Kossuth County, was a town of 3,900 people 50 miles to the east of Spencer. A store in Algona would give the company a consistent presence across north central Iowa. Thomas Kemis, the Spencer native who had moved to Marshall to assist Paul Byers with the store there was named to manage the latest branch. He moved his family to Algona and on June 1, 1935 Arnold Motor Supply opened its new store. With all four stores showing a profit for 1936, the company gained $13,682 on gross sales of $236,542.

Arnold Motor Supply in Sheldon, Iowa, mid 1930's

In 1936, LeRoy Rusch and Florence Pullen decided to get married. Florence was a valuable member of the office and E.P. did not want to lose her, so he brought LeRoy back to the Spencer store where he became manager and worked for the remainder of his career.

Growth of Arnold Motor Supply was not just happening through additional locations. As it became more established, the company was also acquiring rights to sell parts from more manufacturers. Auto part manufacturers were seeing the benefit to selling through smaller jobbers located in smaller towns. That change in the manufacturers' philosophy, coupled with the increasing industry presence of Arnold Motor Supply, gave the branches more options when buying from manufacturers.

The company was also growing in their ability to serve customers through more efficient means of delivery. Starting with the original 1927 Roadster, the company was continually working with an ever-evolving fleet of delivery vehicles, striving for the best solution to deliver what they called "minute man service" to mechanics, garages, and dealers spread across the territory. As they approached the late 1930s, the company had settled on a ton–and-a-quarter Dodge truck with a custom body. The delivery trucks were precision planned and immaculately maintained. The trucks and their drivers were the face of Arnold Motor Supply, so their appearance and functionality were imperative.

Continuing growth in Spencer, plus the need for office space to manage the operations of the outlying branches, soon made it apparent that the company was outgrowing the Peter Ostrom building that had long been its home. The Cornwall Building, just south of the new Spencer Post Office was built specifically for Arnold Motor Supply with enough space to house a spacious store, offices, and the machine shop.

The store covered the front of the building, large windows illuminating a well-organized showroom with steel shelving. Behind the store were four offices, one for E.P. Arnold, one for Robert Byers who did the purchasing for the five stores, a general office for Florence Rusch and the bookkeepers, and a conference room for sales meetings. On the north side of the building was the machine shop which held a piston grinder, a clutch rebuilder, a pinhole grinder, and a paint mixing machine. In the rear was a garage area to park the three delivery trucks that ran routes out of Spencer every day. Arnold Motor Supply left the Ostrom Building for this new home in August of 1938.

To this point, Spencer was the largest city with an Arnold Motor Supply. Aware of the success his old partner was having with Lewis Motor Supply in Waterloo, E.P. wanted to venture into a larger city as well. With a population in 1930 of over 23,000, Mason City, Iowa was significantly larger than the other branch locations. Located 100 miles east of Spencer on US Highway 18, Mason City was in a perfect location to continue the territory to the east. With the Algona branch halfway between Spencer and Mason City, the territories overlapped nicely for the size of sales routes the company liked to run.

Once the company was established and had a large enough pool of talent, E.P. strongly preferred promotion from within whenever possible, especially after the quick exit of L.A. Forbord in 1934. E.P. asked Kieth Byers, who had already managed Spencer and Sheldon, to move to Mason City and assume the role of manager in the new store there. LeRoy Rusch, now married to Florence, became manager of the Spencer store. With Kieth at the helm, the Mason City Arnold Motor Supply opened for business in the fall of 1938.

Relying only on internal capital, Arnold Motor Supply had now grown to five stores over ten years. Each of the store managers also had money invested in their own branch and the company now numbered 25 people. E.P. was quick to share profits and credit with the leaders he had assembled around him. He was adamant that the success of the company was attributable to them, saying, "In our story, you cannot give this group too much credit. I could probably run one store, but when it comes to the others, I could not have organized them or run them had it not been for these people who grew up with me."

Florence Rusch would later say E.P. treated the company like a family in those days. Of course it almost was family. Among the employees at that time were Irene Arnold's three brothers, Kieth, Paul, and Robert Byers, plus Florence Rusch, her husband LeRoy, and two of her brothers: Gib and Harvey Pullen.

Though electricity had been available in the city of Spencer since 1894, rural electrification did not start to gather momentum until the Rural Electrification Act of 1936 provided federal government loans for the installation of systems for rural electrical distribution. Power came to rural Clay County in late 1938 and made a significant change in the way of life for many Arnold Motor Supply customers and employees. Rural electrification opened possibilities beyond just convenience and lighting for Iowa's farmers. It also increased their productivity by allowing for labor- saving machines such as electric water pumps for livestock and irrigation.

On September 1, 1939, Nazi Germany invaded Poland. Once again, war loomed over Europe as Great Britain and France responded to the aggression by declaring war against Germany. While the United States maintained neutrality in the conflict spreading across Europe and the

Pacific, life was changing in Iowa. Newspapers told of battles on an almost daily basis and there was much discussion about the best way for the United States to deal with the growing war. The United States armed forces were building up prior to actual involvement. Bolstered by news of the war in Europe, many young American men sought to enlist in 1939 and 1940. Within Arnold Motor Supply, Florence's brother Gib Pullen left his sales job in Marshall, Minnesota to enlist in the United States Navy.

Despite the uncertainty abroad, E.P. still had his eye on expansion. After calculating profits for January, 1940 at four times those of January, 1939, a cautiously optimistic E.P. sent this memo to his managers: "Here's hoping we don't lose all of it in February. January was sure good." The branch store in Marshall, Minnesota was a lengthy 120 miles north of Spencer. E.P. liked the idea of a Minnesota store in the gap between Spencer and Marshall to provide better coverage of the southern Minnesota territory. The city selected for this new venture was the seat of Martin County. Fairmont, a town of 5,500 was located 70 miles northeast of Spencer. Robert Byers, who had been purchasing for the stores, moved his family to Fairmont to manage the store. On March 13, 1940, the Fairmont, Minnesota branch, Arnold Motor Supply number six, was open for business. At the end of 1940, four of the six stores showed a profit and the company gained $15,000 on $346,000 in sales.

As the United States stood on the brink of the Second World War, Arnold Motor Supply was operating in six locations. Further south and east, E.P.'s friend and former partner B.J. Lewis had followed a similar path, opening branch locations to serve a wider territory around Waterloo. Spencer residents discussed the arrival of Gone with the Wind at the Spencer Theater, billed as the greatest motion picture ever made. The Helsinki Summer Olympics were cancelled due to war in Europe and the University of Minnesota Golden Gopher football team earned a national championship.

The entire company in front of the new Spencer store 1938

9. Mr. Arnold

The 1930s was a decade of tremendous personal transition for E.P. and Irene Arnold. In 1930, they were a married couple without children, living in a small rented home, trying to grow a single store into a successful business. When the decade closed ten years later, they had a child, and the family was living in one of the most beautiful homes in Spencer. They were leaders in the community and E.P. was head of one of the largest businesses in town.

Through it all, the success did not change who E.P. was. Because of his character, he continued to treat the people around him with the same respect he had when he moved to Spencer in 1926. He enjoyed going to the Moose Lodge for lunch with his friends and loved to come out of his office and chat with customers who came into the store.

After Merrill was born in July of 1932, it was soon apparent that his eyesight was significantly below average. He would eventually be declared legally blind, though with his thick glasses he could see well enough to participate in many activities with other children his age. There was concern, however, over his ability to safely cross streets and walk around town as he grew older. Well before Merrill was old enough for school, E.P. and Irene began to plan on building or buying a home of their own.

After the Sheldon store was well established, E.P. was earning a substantial income from the company. This made it possible for him to build a beautiful new home. They selected a location less than a block from Spencer's Lincoln Elementary School. This would allow Merrill to walk there as simply as crossing the street.

E.P. bought a large lot on West 3rd Street in March, 1934, and plans began for a new home. Architect Carl V. Johnson of Des Moines was selected to draw the plans based on his English Tudor designs. Proving as forward-thinking in building his residence as in building his business, E.P. built the first air- conditioned home in Spencer. He also included other modern conveniences such as an automatic dishwasher and a built-in radio aerial system to allow for radio reception in any room. Loads of stone were brought in to decorate the exterior of the house and the beautifully landscaped yard.

Interior design of the home was done by William A French and Company from Minneapolis, Minnesota. Every room in the house followed a color scheme prescribed by the designers. The kitchen was designed to include all the conveniences of the day. The main floor contained a beautifully paneled music room, a formal dining room, and a spacious sunken living room with white carpeting, dark woodwork and a beamed ceiling. The second floor contained a large master bedroom with an adjoining dressing room for Irene, a bedroom for Merrill, and two bathrooms. The basement had a beautiful recreation room with fireplace. There were two staircases: a front staircase leading to the basement recreation room and a second leading to the kitchen for everyday use. On Saturday, September 8, the family moved into the new $20,000 English Tudor home which would instantly become one of the grandest residences in town.

E.P. Arnold did not take his success for granted. Upon moving into the luxurious new home, he wrote a letter to his longest tenured employee, Florence Rusch, thanking her for all she had done over the years to help make the company what it had become. Florence would keep this letter for the rest of her life. E.P. was, without a doubt, the visionary behind the company and its growth but he always referred to "us" rather than "me" when talking about the success of the firm.

Mrs. Arnold was very active in church and social functions. She enjoyed bowling and was an avid golfer. Merrill loved being outdoors and enjoyed singing. E.P. had grown up in a musical family. His brothers would frequently sing for gatherings and his sisters were good musicians, primarily playing the piano. Merrill also had musical interest and sang in choir through high school. He was also involved in speech contests, camera club, and the school play. He went to great lengths to overcome his poor eyesight and did not allow it to be an excuse for not participating in the activities he enjoyed.

When he was a child, Merrill loved horses more than anything else. E.P.'s own upbringing on the farm had given him an appreciation of animals and this was one thing father and son shared through Merrill's life. In July, 1947, fourteen-year-old Merrill showed his prize horse

Indian Chief at the Des Moines National Horse Show. Indian Chief was named winner in the Gaited Championship Stake. Merrill took Indian Chief to shows all over the Midwest with much success.

In 1949 he took Indian Chief to the Missouri State Fair to show in the 4-year old 5-gaited class. There were 16 horses in the ring, with 15 of the entrants being professionals. Merrill, as the only amateur, won the class. Most of the professional riders got off their horses and congratulated him. One newspaper account described Indian Chief as "one of the finest horses in the Midwest". Merrill also loved to show cattle at shows and fairs, a hobby he shared with his father. Merrill would spend the rest of his life riding horses and working outdoors with cattle.

Always a civic minded man, E.P. Arnold was selected by the Spencer mayor to serve on the initial Board of Trustees for the Spencer Municipal Utilities. He served as co-chairman of a committee to raise money for a significant addition to the Spencer Municipal Hospital, and also served as co-chairman of a committee in his church to raise money for a new building. E.P. was a well-respected and well-liked man because of his business acumen and friendly demeanor.

The new Spencer Hospital in 1935

During the steady expansion of the 1930s, E.P. formulated his business principles which would serve him and the company well for the rest of his life. He was a tireless worker with a definite idea of how he wanted things done. Whenever anyone would attribute success to luck, he was known to say, "The harder I've worked, the luckier I've gotten." E.P. expected his employees to work hard as well and always put emphasis on going the extra mile for the customer.

He described his philosophy this way: "I like to think that the philosophy we formulated ...caused this growth. I believe any business should have a creed or things in which it believes. We believe no business has a right to exist unless it serves a purpose in its territory. We believe price is not of importance – someone will always undersell us – but we believe our service is of importance. We believe our responsibility is first to our customers, the sole reason for our existence; then to our employees whom we depend on to serve those customers; and then to the ownership or partners."

He was known as a fair manager who openly communicated company happenings with his partners and employees. Nearly every week he would come into the accounting office, sit down with the bookkeepers and say, "Well, I'd better get you up to date." He would then proceed to fill them in on the state of the business. He was always interested in his employees and their families and would frequently stop to visit with those in his employ about personal matters. These conversations were always genuine and much appreciated by his staff.

While friendly and interested, he also ran a very tight ship, expecting employees to dress very professionally. He did not allow idle talking in the office and employees in the stores and machine shops were not allowed to listen to the radio or even whistle. Employees were expected to be punctual. Everyone in the office arrived at the same time, took a break together and went to lunch at the same time.

As a manager, E.P. was never condescending, seldom showed anger and always let employees know exactly what was expected of them. He believed hiring good people and giving them a stake in the company was the number one key to a successful business. Just a few months before his death, E.P. Arnold put this philosophy into words saying, "I knew if the branch made money it would be because of the branch manager, not me. The manager is the man who makes things happen, and if he owned part of the company, if he had his own money invested, then he would work harder. And if he made it successful, he deserved more than his salary; he deserved part of what the company earned. I've applied that philosophy throughout the company and now everyone is a part owner. You don't build a business with buildings of brick and stone. You build it with people. If they have a part of the company, they work harder and better. And that's what makes the company go."

The Arnolds' English Tudor home

10. World War II

Sunday December 7, 1941 was a mild winter day in western Iowa. The temperature hovered near the freezing point as residents got up in the morning and headed to church. By the time they had returned home and sat down to Sunday dinner, it looked like a beautiful sunny afternoon would bring temperatures into the 50s. Iowans enjoying their noon meals were oblivious that the attack on Pearl Harbor had begun fifteen minutes earlier. One member of the Arnold Motor Supply family was anything but oblivious. Gib Pullen, who had enlisted in 1939, was stationed in Pearl Harbor at the time of the attack. An associated press bulletin arrived at the major news networks shortly after noon, and by 1:30 radio programs were interrupted to bring the news of the attack to the public.

The first eyewitness broadcast arrived later in the afternoon, with a Honolulu reporter broadcasting a brief message. "Hello, NBC. Hello, NBC. This is KTU in Honolulu, Hawaii. I am speaking from the roof of the Advertiser Publishing Company Building. We have witnessed this morning the distant view a brief full battle of Pearl Harbor and the severe bombing of Pearl Harbor by enemy planes, undoubtedly Japanese. The city of Honolulu has also been attacked and considerable damage done. This battle has been going on for nearly three hours. One of the bombs dropped within fifty feet of KTU tower. It is no joke. It is a real war. The public of Honolulu has been advised to keep in their homes and away from the Army and Navy. There has been serious fighting going on in the air and in the sea. The heavy shooting seems to be . . . We cannot estimate just how much damage has been done, but it has been a very severe attack. The Navy and Army appear now to have the air and the sea under control."

By that evening a blackout was in effect on the United States' west coast, as residents feared a possible attack on the mainland. Late the next morning, President Roosevelt delivered his "Day of Infamy" Speech to a joint session of congress while Americans huddled around radios across the country. Within the hour, the United States had declared war against Japan. Three days later Germany and Italy declared war against the United States, and Washington responded in kind. Though preparations and war talk had dominated the nation for several months, there had been some remnant of hope that war could be avoided. That hope was now gone.

The effects of the war were immediate. A flood of young men, enraged by what they viewed as a treacherous attack at Pearl Harbor, overran enlistment centers all across the United States. The economic focus of the nation turned to war production almost overnight. Rationing of food and materials such as rubber and steel changed the lives of every American. Many American businesses were also affected. Men from small town America who did not enter the armed services left for defense manufacturing jobs in larger cities. This had a significant impact on the economy and job market in the smaller towns.

Recycling scrap materials was actively encouraged. In April, 1942, the Des Moines Register published information from the War Production Board: "The steel industry has been rapidly stepping up its production..., but we need to get production up to the industry's full capacity of 90,000,000 tons - a total equal to the output of the rest of the world combined. This volume of production cannot be attained or increased unless an additional 6,000,000 tons of scrap iron and steel is obtained promptly. We are faced with the fact that some steel furnaces have been allowed to cool down and that many of them are operating from day to day and hand to mouth, due only to the lack of scrap.

The rubber situation is also critical. In spite of the recent rubber drive, there is a continuing need for large quantities of scrap rubber. We are collecting every possible pound from the factories, arsenals and shipyards; we are speeding up the flow of material from automobile graveyards; we are tearing up abandoned railroad tracks and bridges, but unless we dig out an additional 6,000,000 tons of steel and great quantities of rubber, copper, brass, zinc and tin, our boys may not get all the fighting weapons they need in time. Even one old shovel will help make 4 hand grenades."

The shortage of rubber resulted in efforts to restrict driving. There was a concerted effort to reduce driving through carpooling and elimination of unnecessary trips.

Publications encouraged driving 35 MPH or slower to conserve wear on tires. The motive behind much of the conservation was not gasoline or automobile parts but rather to lessen the need for rubber. Vehicles were issued gasoline ration stickers that could limit weekly gasoline usage to as little as 4 gallons in non-essential vehicles.

The nation's sudden ramp-up in defense production put an extreme demand on manufacturing facilities. The demand for machine shop equipment far outpaced the ability to manufacture such equipment. Premium prices were paid to anyone willing to sell their machine shop equipment to a defense manufacturer. When the war began, Arnold Motor Supply's machine shop faced competition from four primary machine shops in northern Iowa and southern Minnesota. All four looked at the economic conditions, the rationing and driving restrictions, and the high prices paid for equipment, and made the decision to sell their equipment to defense manufacturers and reduce or eliminate their machine shop capabilities. E.P. Arnold did the opposite.

Just as he had done ten years earlier with the expansion into Sheldon during the depths of the Great Depression, E.P. once again expanded when his peers were contracting. He petitioned the War Production Board for a new Van Norman crankshaft grinder for the Spencer shop. The board had approved production of fifty such machines across the United States and allocated only two to the upper Midwest region. Skeptics asserted there was no way a town the size of Spencer could support this $10,000 piece of equipment. This was no daring move in the face of overwhelming odds. As before, the decision to expand was well thought-out, and supported by a solid understanding of his business.

In March, 1942, E.P. saw pessimism invading every aspect of local business. In response, he wrote a letter to his managers explaining his rationale for optimism. He warned, "I continually hear good sensible men make the statement that there is nothing left for us in Iowa and Minnesota, and that we will all be out of business." In response to this sentiment he made several points. First, as had been the case in the First World War, agriculture was a vital industry for the war effort. He made this case to his managers. "We live in small towns in agricultural districts. People will say to you that we have no defense plants. I say we have thousands of defense plants and that we live in the center of it all. Our defense plants are the thousands of farms producing foods for the war, the most essential item of all. The average farmer, even in normal times, did very little unnecessary driving with his car. There will be less shrinkage in the miles actually driven among the farmers than any other class of people in the United States."

He then laid out five points why he expected their business to continue to thrive.

"1. The price of each part will probably be thirty per cent higher. This means we could sell thirty per cent less parts and yet all of us would make as much money.
2. Your closest competitor for the parts business has always been the car factories. You know the car factories in normal times almost forced their dealers to buy their parts

from them. The car factories now have laid off probably eighty per cent of their men. Even if the car factories have parts to deliver, they have very little contact with the dealer now and certainly have no way to force the dealer to buy parts from them.

3. You have less and less competition each week from other jobbers. Smaller jobbers will either fail completely or take their men off the road and discontinue the use of trucks. You must, and can, get a greater percent of the business that is being done in your territory.

4. Statistics show for years that the first year a car is on the road, we get practically no business from it. The second year we start to sell some parts for it. The third and fourth years we reach the peak of the amount of parts used on that car. In the fifth year there are less parts bought for it. Finally the car is dropped from the list.

In 1942 the "peak year cars" will be the 1938 and 1939 models. All of the records show that there were so many more 1938 and 1939 cars sold than there were 1935 and 1936 cars, that if 1942 was a normal year, the parts business would naturally increase twenty-five per cent. This would mean that even though there is a shrinkage in miles driven, there might still be a demand almost equal to 1941.

5. This will be the best year we have ever had to sell tractor parts. Implement dealers will not be able to keep stocks on hand, especially of tractor sleeves, and if they do have them, they will not give any garage man a discount. Increase your tractor parts sales!"

E.P. closed his letter with a reminder. "You are living in the best spot in the world. Get busy and get a greater per cent of the total business to be had. Do some real sane thinking and don't let these rumors 'get you down'."

E.P. was right to point his sales force toward tractor parts. The early 1940s saw a dramatic movement toward the use of tractors on Iowa's farms. Nationwide, the number of tractors in use on farms rose from 1.6 million in 1940 to 2.4 million just five years later. This growth, coupled with the increased demand for agricultural products during the war, led to a new market that the company left mostly untapped in the years leading up to the war.

When Arnold Motor Supply received authorization for the crankshaft grinder, they also got a priority rating for a new connecting rod and bearing insert grinder. E.P. had a 1,200 square-foot addition built onto the machine shop to house the new equipment. Now he faced another challenge: finding and retaining men to operate the machines. With the exodus of men to armed service and defense manufacturing jobs, there were few prospects for hiring new people to run the machines.

Early on, E.P. recognized the importance of the machine shop to the success of the stores, calling the shops the heart of the business. The Spencer branch had four employees able to do machine shop work: the store manager LeRoy Rusch, his assistant manager Marvin Randall, 19 year old Gar Odor (who had once ridden his bike twenty miles to ask E.P. for a job), and a new hire named Lorol Cleghorn.

During World War II, the Selective Service categorized men into four broad categories. Category I was defined as "Available for Service", Category II was "Deferred because of occupational status", Category III was "Deferred because of dependents", and Category IV was "Deferred specifically by law or because unfit for military service". Gar was classified IV-F (physically unfit) and Lorol was married with two young boys whose draft classification was II-A (deferred for national interest). When LeRoy came up for draft in the fall of 1942 he was given six months deferment due to the importance of Arnold Motor Supply to the agriculture industry. This was intended to give the company enough time to train Marvin Randall so he could operate the equipment in the machine shop when LeRoy was drafted.

Unfortunately these plans were interrupted by tragedy. Paul Byers in Marshall had spent the later part of 1942 battling illness. Doctors advised him to get rest for the sake of his health. On January 25, 1943 he passed away of a heart attack at the age of 34. He left behind his wife of 11 years, Ruth and their 7 year old son Dick. Paul was not only E.P.'s business partner, he was Irene's brother and his death was felt by both the company and the family.

Needing someone to run the Marshall store, E.P. asked LeRoy and Florence to go to Marshall temporarily to keep things running until a permanent replacement could be named. The only person in the company E.P. felt was qualified to become a manager was Marvin Randall who had been groomed to take over the Spencer store. E.P. sent Sheldon manager Seymour Easthouse to Marshall, and Marvin Randall took Seymour's place in Sheldon. E.P. issued an affidavit to the Draft Board asking for another deferment for LeRoy, citing the War Production Board decision to grant priority status for the crankshaft grinder as evidence of the importance of the operation to agriculture and transportation in the area. The Draft Board agreed and LeRoy was allowed to stay in Spencer to keep the operation running.

The new Van Norman crankshaft grinder arrived in December of 1943. The large plate glass windows across the front of the store had to be removed to get the huge machine into the building. With no other crankshaft grinders within 100 miles, the machine frequently operated for 20 hours a day to keep up with the work that poured in from surrounding communities. E.P.'s decision to pursue the crankshaft grinder proved correct and the machine generated significant profit for the company during the duration of its time in service.

Local newspapers delivered news from the war daily, sometimes good news but mostly bad. Almost every day a new local soldier was listed as killed or missing in action. Occasionally families would get a cable from a prisoner of war who had been missing in action and the newspaper would rejoice with the parents to find the son alive. Stories of battle were always in the headlines.

D-Day, June 6th was the beginning of the end for Nazi Germany. As 1944 ground on, the local headlines had a definite turn toward the positive. By August papers and newsreels spoke of retreating Nazis, Patton's advance, and recapturing Paris. The end of war in Europe was within sight. At home, optimistic planning was beginning for celebration of the coming Nazi surrender.

As the war entered its final stages, Arnold Motor Supply was preparing for two new stores. They selected locations in Carroll and Boone Iowa for the seventh and eighth branches. On August 25, 1944 allied armies were able to retake the French capital of Paris. One week later, the store in Carroll was open for business. Harvey Pullen, who had been with the company since 1937, went to Carroll to manage the new store. Carroll had a population of 5,400, was 90 miles south of Spencer, and was the county seat of Carroll County.

Harvey Pullen and Gar Odor in front of the new Carroll, Iowa store in 1944

The following spring, Adolph Hitler took his own life on April 30, 1945, and on May 7, Germany surrendered to the western Allies. Later that same month in the Pacific, Allied troops took Okinawa, the last island before Japan. On August 6 and 9, the United States dropped atomic bombs on Hiroshima and Nagasaki, effectively ending

World War II. Japan officially surrendered on September 2, 1945 and the next month, on October 11, Arnold Motor Supply opened the Boone store. George Ahlers, who had spent three years in the Marshall store moved to manage the latest location.

Boone was typical of the towns E.P. preferred for branches, though larger than most. It was the county seat of Boone County, with a population of around 12,000, located 140 miles southeast of Spencer. The Boone and Carroll territories complemented each other nicely, with the two towns about 50 miles apart. Together, they were a logical addition to the company, as they helped Arnold Motor Supply fill in more territory south of Spencer.

As the country embarked on post-war life, Arnold Motor Supply was well established with eight locations strategically located across northwest Iowa and southwest Minnesota, almost exclusively in medium-sized county seat towns. All were managed by men who had been brought up within the company with at least three years of experience at a store before being moved into management. All the managers were also investors in the company, whose compensation was determined by the profitability of the store.

Along with the growth, E.P. Arnold also saw a disturbing trend inside his company. As with any organization, as the company grew larger there was less direct contact between Arnold and individual employees. The culture he had established in Spencer and spread to the early stores was not reaching the newer members of the company to his satisfaction. E.P. had very high expectations for everyone in the company; a work ethic that was non-negotiable. As America emerged from the Second World War with a newfound strength, Arnold Motor Supply was emerging as well. The company needed guidance from its founder to keep it on track doing the things that had led to success over its first twenty years.

As the 1940s were drawing to a close, E.P. wanted to tighten up the organization. As part of that effort, he composed this letter and sent it out to the leadership across the company:

April 19, 1949

BRANCH MANAGERS AND SALESMEN:
During the past ten years, the trend has been for salesmen to work less hours and less days per week. The same trend has been for business houses to open their doors at a later hour in the morning. Some of our branches have gone along with this idea and, frequently, we are surprised to find how far they have gone with the idea.

I have taken the attitude that, if a top salesman could turn in enough business by working five days per week, then it was certainly O.K. for him to work five days. On the other hand, I have very definite ideas about a new salesman who is trying to develop a new territory or who is trying to develop himself, and then thinks he can do it in five days. For this same reason, I might feel that if a top branch could get the job done and have high sales by opening their doors at 8:00 a.m., it might be O.K. When we go to branches and find the new branches opening at 8:00 a.m. and the old established branches opening at 7:00 or 7:30 a.m., it looks just backwards to me.

All branches should open their doors at 7:30 and quite a lot of the time even earlier. Cleghorn loads his truck at night, and is in his truck and on the road at 7:00 a.m. every morning. I don't believe any of our new or low salesmen can improve on this system. I don't believe any salesman should be around our store after 7:30 a.m.

I believe all new salesmen, who are trying to develop a territory should be out on the territory at least 5 1/2 days. When I mention 5 1/2 days, I don't mean 11:00 a.m. Saturday, but believe you should be on your territory until approximately 1:30 p.m. This would give you about four hours Saturday P.M. to work on your catalogue or clean up your truck. There is no reason why you new or low salesmen should think that you could earn your living in five days.

It has been surprising to us, because the branches and the salesmen who have gone to the extreme on hours and days, are quite often the lowest ones in sales, or the new ones.

IF THE SHOE FITS, PUT IT ON. THERE WILL BE NO EASY WAY TO MAKE A LIVING!!!!

E. P. A.

11. Post War

In July, 1944, optimism was on the rise among the Allied nations for a successful conclusion to the war. Representatives from each Allied nation met in Bretton Woods, New Hampshire for the United Nations Monetary and Financial Conference. During this conference, all attending nations agreed to adopt monetary policy that would tie their currency to the U.S. dollar in order to regulate international exchange rates and foster international trade. The fact this meeting was held in the United States and chose U.S. currency as the international standard was a striking sign that the United States had replaced the United Kingdom as the world's dominant financial power.

The Bretton Woods system successfully established a stable international monetary system which allowed the United States to more easily sell goods to war-ravaged Europe. Since much of the productive capabilities of Europe had been destroyed by the war, the United States directly benefitted from the rebuilding effort by exporting goods to Europeans. The Bretton Woods system was largely based on lessons learned in the aftermath of the First World War, where drastic fluctuations in currency exchange rates greatly hampered international trade and contributed to the economic difficulties in rural America.

In Iowa, the contrast between the years following World War I and those following World War II was striking. Rather than a dramatic drop in demand as had been the case in 1919, exports to Europe flourished. Rural Iowans celebrated liberation from nearly thirty years filled with economic depression and two world wars. The result was an explosion of marriages, entrepreneurship, business expansion and the beginning of the baby boom. The United States was entering the golden age of capitalism and enjoying its new found place as the most powerful nation in the world.

One of the great symbols of post war America was the automobile. The number of registered vehicles in Iowa had dropped each year from 1940 to 1945. In December, 1943, 2.59 million families nationwide had "purchasing an automobile" at the top of the list of things they intended to do after the war. With the conclusion of the war, the economic expansion was reflected in the number of cars on Iowa roads. Registrations jumped from less than 700,000 in 1945, a number that was actually fewer than when Arnold Motor Supply began eighteen years earlier, to over one million in 1950, an increase of 54% over that five year span.

Of course life wasn't perfect after the axis powers surrendered. On October 19, 1945, George Orwell published an essay entitled "You and the Atomic Bomb," in which he introduced a term that would shape the next 45 years of world history. The term was "Cold War." Orwell defined the invention of the atomic bomb as an influence on the world that would, "put an end to large-scale wars at the cost of prolonging indefinitely a peace that is no peace." The Cold War served as the damper to the enthusiasm and optimism of the post war years in America.

Arnold Motor Supply closed out the 1940s with another branch opening in Oelwein, Iowa in the fall of 1946. As the company extended father east than ever before, Mervell Russell moved from the Mason City store where had had worked for two years, to take over management of the ninth Arnold Motor Supply. Oelwein was the largest town in Fayette County in northeast Iowa, with a population of 7,800. At a distance of 200 miles east, Oelwein was considerably farther from Spencer than any other store, and was nearly 100 miles away from its nearest sister branch in Mason City. Gar Odor, who had moved from Spencer to Carroll in 1946, moved again in March, 1949, when he was promoted to manager of the Oelwein branch.

The company inaugurated the 1950s by opening store number ten in Marshalltown, Iowa in November, 1950. Florence Rusch's brother Ray Pullen had started with the company in the Carroll store in 1946 and he now moved to Marshalltown to manage the new branch. Fifty five miles east of Boone, Marshalltown expanded the territory farther east and south, continuing the trend of moving to the largest town in a county and keeping branches at a reasonable distance from each other. For 23 years, the company had been growing at a steady rate of a new store every other year. The addition of the tenth store would bring an end to new store expansion for the next twelve years.

In the spring of 1950, E.P. contacted nearby Everly High School seeking a recommendation for a book-keeper. The school recommended a senior named Joyce Wagner. Joyce was interviewed by Mr. Arnold, was offered the job, and began what would be a nearly 58 year career with the company. The next month, the United States began involvement in the Korean War. The Forgotten War, as it has been called, did not generate a lot of public attention primarily because it followed so closely on the heels of the much larger Second World War. The conflict in Korea lasted from June 1950 until July of 1953.

Six months after starting her new career, Joyce was married. When her husband Dean entered the armed forces, he was stationed in Washington state while waiting to be sent overseas to Korea. Every evening he would place a collect call to Joyce, not knowing what day he would have to leave the country. Every day Mr. Arnold would ask Joyce if she had heard from Dean the night before, knowing that when the calls stopped, Dean had been deployed overseas. When the calls did stop nearly a month later, Joyce had tallied a substantial phone bill. That month E.P. gave her a check for $100 to cover phone charges, telling Joyce that Dean's service to the country was surely worth that much.

It had become customary to bring all the store managers together every year, usually in January, to discuss the business of the previous year. E.P. wanted to change the format of this meeting to encourage more communication between the ten stores. A few months after the inauguration of Dwight Eisenhower as president, the company held its annual meeting. In this letter to the store managers he described his vision for the 1953 meeting.

"About once each year we have a sales meeting together. Really, we have this mostly so we can entertain all of you with a dinner and we can all visit together. It always seems to be my job to try and talk to you, and it must become tiresome always hearing the same person with the same line of chatter.
There must be many times, throughout the year, when all of you have things come up about which you would like to ask why do we do things this way? why can't we do this or that? what about our prices? This year we would like to try a meeting in which everything was wide open for you to shoot the questions, We want all of your criticism from it we hope to gain useful information.
I promise you I will not embarass [sic] anyone. I will try to answer your questions. To make this meeting a success we need to be sure that you men will speak up in open discussion. It will be a flop if you do not do your part.
Let's try it we want constructive criticism."

E.P. was certainly interested in the opinions of his employees and partners. He was also interested in their lives. His people-centric style, mixed with his analytical accountant's mind, made him an effective leader and communicator. People in the company knew that E.P. genuinely cared. He recognized the value of people and treated everyone with respect which, in turn, gained him much respect.

E.P. and Irene Arnold at the 1951 company Christmas party

As automobile and home purchases skyrocketed through the early fifties, there became a need for better infrastructure to move people from their suburban homes to jobs in the cities. In 1956, the federal government passed the Interstate Highway Act which provided for construction of over 40,000 miles of freeway over ten years. The development of interstate highways and suburban living was a boon to some areas of the country. However, many rural areas were deprived of shopping revenue as increased mobility caused travelers to bypass smaller towns. Farm population shrank by 17% during the decade, as people left rural America for higher paying urban jobs.

In the 1950s, the focus of company growth and investment at Arnold Motor Supply shifted away from new locations toward construction of new buildings for the various branches. When the tenth store in Marshalltown was added, the company was renting all ten locations. The move toward building ownership progressed at the same steady pace that expansion had, with the company constructing a new building every other year. By the beginning of 1958, the Algona, Marshalltown, Carroll, and Oelwein stores were in new company-owned buildings and construction was underway for an impressive new facility to house the Spencer store and the corporate offices.

As 1959 drew to a close, the company had acquired three parcels of land ready for construction. They bought lots in Sheldon and Marshall on which they would build new buildings. They also bought a large tract of land in south Spencer where construction began on a new 26,000 square foot warehouse. E.P. believed the company was now big enough to benefit from pooling purchases for the ten stores into a single location. With the new warehouse facility, full truckloads of parts could be purchased by the warehouse and then delivered on regular routes from the warehouse to the individual stores. Gib Pullen, who had returned to the company in 1945 upon his discharge from the Navy, was selected to manage the new warehouse. The transition from a chain of stores to a warehousing and distribution operation opened a completely new set of opportunities and challenges for Arnold Motor Supply.

Kieth Byers and LeRoy Rusch with Kieth's airplane

12. Arnold Angus

When Merrill graduated from High School in 1950, he spent a year in college and then returned to Spencer with his mind made up; he wanted to be a farmer. Since his first horse show at the age of 13, he loved working with animals. His farm career began during 1951 on a small three acre plot, purchased several years earlier by E.P., inside the Spencer city limits. This land contained a large cattle barn where Merrill started raising pure-bred cattle.

In the fall of 1951, E.P. purchased 210 acres of farmland ten miles south of Spencer. The following spring he was able to purchase adjoining land. This farm proved to be an ideal location for Merrill to pursue his dream of farming. He moved to the farm. The barn in Spencer was cut into sections and moved to the farm with him. Here, Merrill began to steadily grow his herd of Black Angus cattle. From his small hobby beginnings in Spencer, his herd grew to 60 head of cattle by 1958. He planned to continue to grow his herd with a goal of 80 head.

The cattle business was Merrill's love and was actually E.P.'s love as well. E.P. sold auto parts because he was good at business and saw great opportunity in auto parts. He worked on the farm because he loved it. His progressive outlook toward business carried over to his approach to farming. Both E.P. and Merrill looked for ways to increase efficiency and improve production. They were interested in automation of tasks and processes to improve breeding and weight gain in their cattle. In addition to his interest in livestock, Merrill was very interested in the mechanical aspects of farm life, and worked on diesel engines and other aspects of his farm machinery.

By the mid-1950s, E.P. was so involved with Black Angus cattle that he served as President of the Iowa State Angus Association. He traveled across the Midwest speaking to audiences of cattlemen, and meeting with experts and academics on behalf of the association. Merrill would frequently attend livestock shows across the Midwest. E.P. would occasionally accompany him when his schedule would allow it. E.P. was growing into a dual role as both businessman and farmer. Perfect Circle Corporation published an auto parts trade magazine called Jobber Journal. The Summer, 1959 issue pictured E.P. on the front cover showing prize bull Black Conquestor in front of one of the Arnolds' cattle barns, perfectly illustrating the dual life of E.P. Arnold.

The father and son pair continued to grow Arnold Angus Farm by implementing industry developments to further production capabilities. By the 1970s, with the addition of a second farm five miles to the west, the farming operation had grown to nearly 1,500 acres of land split between raising corn and alfalfa and pasture land for grazing. Merrill's original goal of 80 head was obliterated as his herd eventually grew to 900 Black Angus cattle. The

Arnolds employed 16 grain silos to store feed for the large herd. Electric augers and conveyer belts enabled Merrill or his hired hands to feed and check 360 cows in an hour.

All of the corn used to feed the cattle was grown by Merrill. He also grew some alfalfa for hay but had to purchase semi-loads of hay throughout the year. The fieldwork was done with two of the latest John Deere four-wheel-drive tractors. In order to keep the operation running, the Arnolds hired two full-time hands plus frequent seasonal help. In his later years, once he was semi-retired from the partnership, E.P. spent more and more time with Merrill on the farm doing what he loved.

E.P. Arnold with his prize Angus bull Black Conquestor in 1959

13. Building

After 23 years living in the English Tudor home E.P. and Irene built in 1934, the couple decided to build another new home and move to a more scenic rural setting. In 1957, they built a sprawling brick ranch home on the western-most outskirts of Spencer, overlooking the Little Sioux River. They sold the Tudor home to funeral director Milt Warner, who built a chapel off the living room and converted the beautiful house into a funeral home in 1958. The Arnolds' new location had a wide lawn and the house's many large windows overlooked a grassy meadow dotted with wildflowers running down to the river's edge. They placed feeders in the yard to attract birds and were frequently visited by deer heading to and from the river.

While working on his new home, E.P. turned his attention to a new home for the company. Arnold Motor Supply had grown over the first thirty years of its history from a single store to a thriving ten store enterprise. The new building being constructed in Spencer during 1958 was indicative of the company's increased status. E.P. Arnold designed much of the building himself, desiring the first floor to house the store and machine shop with the general offices for the company on the second floor.

E.P. specifically wanted a lot of glass across the front of the store to present a well-lit, comfortable showroom. This was in direct contrast to many auto parts stores of the day which typically did not place high priority on presentation. E.P., with his roots in grocery sales was more in tune with product presentation than a typical parts store owner would be. He insisted on a clean, well-organized store to "take the parts business out of the dark and grease" that customers so often encountered in competitors' stores.

In addition to the glass front, the attractive showroom was paneled with light colored wood and had large windows that allowed customers to see into the machine shop located adjacent to the sales counter. Behind the counter were doors leading to aisles of auto parts and an office for LeRoy Rusch, the store manager. In the back of the store were garage doors for the delivery trucks and a separate counter for salesmen to work from when completing paperwork or readying their trucks for the next route.

The prevailing modernist architectural style of the 1950s typically utilized a lot of glass and stainless steel. Ascribing to the theory that less is more when it comes to ornamentation, buildings of this style typically feature clean lines and open spaces. The new home of Arnold Motor Supply fit well into this style. The exterior was a mixture of glass, sandstone, and light colored brick. Adjacent to the main entrance showroom doors in the front of the store was a separate entrance that housed the elevator and stairway leading upstairs to the offices. Fixtures and railings were made of stainless steel. A glass wall with glass doors separated the landing at the top of the stairs from the main Arnold Motor Supply offices. A long hallway led along the side of the building to more office suites in the back. These were rented out to various professionals.

Two large paneled offices dominated the front of the second floor overlooking the street, with a smaller conference room between them. The first office inside the glass doors was occupied by Kieth Byers who was General Manager over all the store operations. The large corner office was occupied by E.P. Arnold, with Florence Rusch at the end of the hall in the office next to E.P. Other offices were used for Accounts Payable, the mimeograph machine and other business equipment. A large room toward the back of the complex housed the bookkeepers, with a room behind them for filing. The overall appearance of the corporate offices was impressive and professional, yet efficient and comfortable. The building exhibited excellent planning and design, with an eye toward future expansion.

New store and company offices in 1958

With the new store and main office completed, E.P. once again turned his focus to building the warehouse in south Spencer. While the new main office building was built for style and function, the new warehouse was all about function. Consistent with his focus on people and doing things with excellence, E.P. made a unique design decision for the warehouse. On a typical warehouse, loading docks allow trailers to back up to a door so warehouse personnel could load or unload the trailer. In the Spencer warehouse, E.P. installed garage doors to allow trucks to back all the way into the warehouse. This allowed the trucks to be docked at inside loading docks, which was extremely helpful during the cold winter months. Warehouse employees could work inside while loading or unloading. Semi-trailers would have a chance to thaw and de-ice, which made coupling and uncoupling much easier for drivers. The original warehouse had internal docks for one

106

semi-trailer and two straight trucks. In 1968, the warehouse was nearly doubled in size and two more inside docks were added to accommodate semi-trailers.

E.P. Arnold behind the counter of the new Spencer store

14. Anti-Trust Concerns

With the passing of the Sherman Antitrust Act in 1890 the federal government entered into the business of protecting competition in the marketplace. The initial intent of this effort was to ensure businesses did not use unethical means to stifle competition to the detriment of consumers. In 1914 congress extended the efforts to ensure a competitive marketplace by passing the Clayton Act. Section 2 of the Clayton Act was amended in 1936 by the Robinson-Patman Act which among other things specifically addressed price discrimination. Criticized from the beginning for its ambiguous language and structure the act was described by the Supreme Court as "complicated and vague in itself and even more so in its context".

Robinson-Patman was birthed during the Great Depression with the emergence of large grocery store chains. Small independent grocery stores lobbied congress to stop the large chains from using their superior buying power to gain competitive advantage. Robinson-Patman attempted to accomplish this by prohibiting a seller from selling commodity items at different prices to different buyers. Critics argued the law was not only hard to interpret but also fundamentally flawed since anti-trust legislation was supposed to be designed to protect the consumer but Robinson-Patman instead was designed to protect one type of retailer from another with the ultimate result being higher prices to the consumer and less competition.

Because of its ambiguity, over time the philosophy of the Federal Trade Commission on how to enforce Robinson-Patman varied greatly. According to Joshua F. Greenburg in the Antitrust Law Journal, "In the 1950s and 1960s, there was an avalanche of complaints by the Federal Trade Commission against sellers alleging violations of Sections 2(a),(c),(d) and (e). The toy industry, the automotive parts industry and the garment industry were among those that were particular lightning rods for the FTC's wrath. The result was overwhelming condemnation by academics, economists and the organized bar, and almost uniform applause by the courts."

In the early 1960s FTC cases within the automotive parts industry were catching the attention of the leadership at Arnold Motor Supply in light of the new warehouse in Spencer. In 1960 there was American Motor Specialties Co., Inc., Et Al., v. Federal Trade Commission. In 1961 there was MID-SOUTH DISTRIBUTORS et al. and Cotton States, Inc., et al., v. FEDERAL TRADE COMMISSION. In 1962 courts heard Alhambra Motor Parts et al. v. Federal Trade Commission.

Of particular interest was the Alhambra Motor Parts case. The case involved a group of fifty nine auto parts stores in southern California who had combined to form Southern California Jobbers, Inc. (SCJ), a separate company which performed warehousing for the fifty nine stores. The FTC had ruled that SCJ was in violation of Robinson-Patman. In fighting this ruling, the petitioners in this case differentiated between two distinct operations performed by the group, those operations being brokerage and warehousing. Brokerage operations consisted of individual members placing orders with manufacturers under the name of SCJ. The manufacturers would then drop ship these orders directly to the individual member, or allow the SCJ delivery service to combine multiple orders and delivery to members. In contrast, warehouse operations consisted of SCJ ordering, and stocking in its warehouse, forty lines of merchandise in anticipation of future orders from the individual members stores. Since SCJ was providing warehousing and reselling functions for the manufacturers they were given a redistribution discount ranging from 20-28%.

Section 2(c) prohibits a brokerage arrangement where the broker performs no actual service for the seller and the brokerage fee is merely a hidden price discount. Lawyers for SCJ did not contest the findings of the FTC and admitted that the brokerage portion of the business was in violation of Robinson-Patman. However, they did argue that the warehouse portion of the business was not in violation. The act allows for a different price due to "differences in the cost of manufacture, sale, or delivery resulting from the differing methods or quantities". They correctly stated that the warehouse was providing a legitimately valuable service to manufacturers by warehousing their products and then reselling and delivering to jobber stores.

Since the SCJ warehouse was a separate entity from the stores, performing a legitimate function for the sellers and since independent jobbers who competed with the member stores were free to buy from any other warehouse operation, there was no violation of Robinson-Patman. As a result in 1963 the court set aside that portion of the FTC order that pertained to those products where SCJ performed actual warehouse-distributor functions.

Seeing this result, it was decided the best way to keep operations of the Arnold Motor Supply Warehouse compliant with the current FTC interpretation of the law would be to split the warehouse operations apart into a completely separate company. Under that arrangement, the newly formed warehouse company could provide distinct warehouse-distributor functions completely separate from the jobbing functions provided by the individual stores. Investments of those partners associated with the warehouse operation were moved to the newly created partnership which E.P. named The Merrill Company, after his son.

In January of 1964 E.P. issued this notice about the new company at the annual sales meeting, "During the last six months of 1963 much work was done organizing and setting up the beginning of the new warehouse distributing company known as The Merrill Company. The company has been recognized and accepted by all major suppliers as a warehouse distributor. This completes another step in the growth and expansion of our company. It opens the field to further expansion for branches of Arnold Motor Supply. There is a great future for young men in the automotive distribution field, and especially with our company. We are constantly looking for the right ones. The requirement is WORK – are you willing to go beyond requirements?"

Gib Pullen, E.P. Arnold and a Wagner Brake representative in front of the warehouse

15. Transition and Turmoil

The 1960s was a turbulent decade in America and in many ways Arnold Motor Supply reflected that turbulence. Within the company the decade was a mixture of growth and shake up. Since adding the last of the post-war stores at Marshalltown, Iowa in 1950 there had been no new branches and Arnold Motor Supply remained at ten locations. Focus was instead on building new buildings for existing branches. Times were getting a little more difficult for independent auto parts stores as the post war boom began to subside. Many independent store owners began to realize they could not effectively compete with larger chains and looked to sell their businesses.

Location eleven was added with the acquisition of Childs Auto Parts, an existing business in Oskaloosa, Iowa. It became an Arnold Motor Supply on August 13, 1962. Lyle Welsh had been a salesman at the Oelwein store since 1957. With the acquisition, Lyle was promoted to manage the Oskaloosa store and Gar Odor, Oelwein store manager, hired a young car salesman named Larry Wegner to take Lyle's place.

Located forty miles south of Spencer on U.S. Highway 71, Storm Lake, Iowa had long been considered an ideal candidate for an Arnold Motor Supply Store. It was the perfect distance from Spencer, the county seat of Buena Vista County, and filled in the territory nicely between Spencer and Carroll. The company bought ground and built a new building for the twelfth store, which opened in February, 1963. Milo Huddleston transferred from Carroll to manage the newest location. Seven months later President Kennedy was assassinated in Dallas, TX and Lyndon Johnson was sworn in as President.

In 1965, six months after the first U.S. Marines entered Vietnam, the company again turned to acquisition. This time they purchased Roberson's Inc., which had stores in Ames and nearby Nevada. This purchase was a departure from the company's typical preference for locations. Normally, stores were at least forty miles apart to provide for an efficient overlap of sales territory. Ames and Nevada, however, were only nine miles apart and Ames was only 14 miles from the store in Boone. There was much discussion on whether three stores within 23 miles of each other was a practical use of resources. It was soon apparent that the territory could support the stores, and a new building was built at Ames in 1968.

In addition to the new store built for Ames, the company built new buildings in Sheldon in 1960, Marshall in 1962, and Mason City and Oelwein in 1964. These efforts contributed greatly to the building initiative and by the end of the decade, eight of the thirteen stores were in new company-owned buildings.

By the end of 1964, E.P. Arnold was 65 years old. There was growing concern within the company for how much longer he would be able to lead and who would take over when he was no longer able. E.P. himself was also keenly aware of the need to find a successor. He earnestly wanted to ensure the business that he had built through most of his adult life would live on when he was no longer there to lead it. E.P. was looking for someone fifteen to twenty years younger than himself who was an effective leader and had significant experience within the company.

In November, E.P. traveled to Oelwein for the Grand Opening of the newly constructed building there. The Oelwein store manager, Gar Odor was high on the list of potential successors E.P. had in mind. He watched Gar very closely during the preparation and execution of the Grand Opening and came away convinced that Gar would be the one he would groom to take the reins of the company. E.P. had identified his choice to lead the organization but he was not ready to step down just yet. Gar was not everyone's pick, including a few partners who saw themselves running the company. As a result, the last half of the 1960s was as tumultuous inside the company as it was across the nation.

E.P. greets customers at the Oelwein store Grand Opening

The first episode of discontent during this period started in 1965. By this time, the Merrill Company warehouse in Spencer had been operational for five years but employees had not seen a pay raise during that time. The lack of raises fostered frustration among the staff who approached manager Gib Pullen about the situation. Gib spoke with E.P. about the matter and the employees were given pay increases. However, the seeds of discontent were not easily uprooted.

Workers at a local grocery store a few blocks down the street from The Merrill Company had recently joined a union. Impressed with the improvements the union secured for the grocery employees, some Merrill Company workers approached the union about representation. For the next several months there was much discussion between warehouse workers and union representatives. Of course, E.P. and Gib watched these talks with much interest.

One of the employees in the Merrill Company warehouse was Galen Groth, who had grown up just south of Spencer next door to the farm operated by E.P. and Merrill. Galen would frequently do work on the farm, helping to unload hay or perform other farm labor. Galen came to work at the warehouse in 1963 and continued to help on the farm as well. As a testament to both E.P.'s work ethic and love of the farm, he was still very active in the manual labor of farming and would not shy away from throwing hay bales alongside his hired help well into the 1960s. This gave E.P. opportunities to talk to Galen about the benefits the warehouse staff saw in unionizing.

E.P. was adamantly opposed to unionization. He felt that if the day came when he could no longer talk directly with one of his people about their pay or performance, it was the day he would no longer want to be in business. Bob Black, who began a 47-year career with the company in 1953, would later compliment E.P. on his accessibility, saying "He was CEO of the company and a guy like me had access to him any time, 24 hours a day. If you wanted to call him up at home he was willing to talk to you, to tell you what you should do. He was a very nice gentleman."

This personal interaction was very important to E.P. and something he enjoyed very much. He bristled when union officials objected to him talking to employees during union negotiations. It was frequently said that if you were a hard

117

worker, E.P. liked you. Of course, the implication was that he didn't have much patience with those he felt did not work hard. E.P. was a firm believer in individual accountability and felt everyone worked harder when they were rewarded directly for the results of their labor. He feared collective bargaining would take that away, and he felt that would be detrimental to the entire organization.

Except for the brief period of incorporation in the very early days, the company had always operated as a partnership. Initially the partners were just the store managers, but E.P. had already started to include the best salesmen and shop employees as partners as early as the 1940s. In 1966 he decided the best way to avoid unionization of his employees was to offer them all an opportunity to join the partnership. The partnership required a minimum investment of $500, an homage to the $500 E.P. himself had invested in 1927. Recognizing this would be a challenge for many, he offered to give them the $500. This proved to be an attractive offer and every employee accepted.

At that point, it was mandated in the partnership agreement that anyone who came to work for the company had to invest as a partner. He saw this move as an effective way to eliminate the threat of unionization and at the same time benefit those who worked for him. He summed up his philosophy this way, "They believe that what happens to the company really affects them. And of course, they are right. I don't know of any other firm with higher morale or people working for it who are as diligent and loyal as ours."

Opening the partnership ended the union discussion since everyone was now an owner, but it created a new set of challenges. The Department of Labor raised concerns about the legality of the partnership. Since everyone in the company was now a partner, they were all considered self-employed which meant the company was no longer withholding any income taxes. E.P. and the company's legal counsel, Louis S. Goldberg, traveled to Kansas City to meet with representatives from the Department of Labor and the IRS who questioned the structure of the company. Ultimately they were able to show the legality of the partnership and the issue was put to rest.

The company now turned attention to a more positive project: planning the 40th Anniversary Celebration, which would be held in April, 1967. Much of the planning for the program was delegated to Marshall manager Harvey McVey, Marshalltown manager Ray Pullen, and Gar Odor who had transferred to manage the Ames and Nevada stores when they were acquired in 1965. True to form, E.P. issued a directive to these men as the planning began, "I think the story should be around the founding of a company, not the founding of an individual, because I think many individuals made up the company."

E.P. used the occasion to reiterate his belief in the partnership and his appreciation for his friend Louis Goldberg. He had this statement printed in the anniversary program. "For forty years I have believed that a Partnership was the best way to set up a business so that all parties involved furnished capital and services and that they all shared in net profits. I was fortunate 35 years ago, when I met Mr. Louis S. Goldberg of Sioux City, and he became our C.P.A and Legal Counselor and he also believed in partnerships. Arnold Motor Supply is now owned and operated by 130 partners and The Merrill Company is owned and operated by 24 partners. I believe that we all contributed and have received benefits from that Partnership belief and trust. I would not want to set up a business in any other way, and I enjoy working with my Partners and shall continue to work with you as long as my health permits."

The 1967 annual meeting, in addition to celebrating the 40th anniversary of the company, was very much like the meetings they held every year. Presentations were given by Ray Pullen to the top city salesmen, territory salesmen, and machine shop men. Harvey McVey updated the company on land purchases, building construction and other projects, and Gar Odor reviewed the history of the company.

The last speech of the day was titled "Yesterday, Today, Tomorrow" and was delivered by E.P. The speech was uncharacteristically emotional for E.P., perhaps because he knew his time was winding down. He addressed the issue of his replacement simply by stressing that the leadership the company would need in the future was there in form of the partners who had invested a portion of their lives into the partnership. After the meeting was done, he wrote a letter to Ray Pullen thanking him for his contribution to the event in which he stated, "There has been too much concern about my replacement. I do not like to talk about it or hear about it. The material that the company needs was in the room that night." E.P. was now like a proud father watching his company grow up and gain independence.

The following winter, the Department of Labor was again involved with the company. In January, 1968 an injunction was filed against Arnold Motor Supply and E.P. Arnold in U.S. District Court. The Department of Labor charged the company with violating over-time and record keeping requirements of the Fair Labor Standards Act. The suit alleged that Arnold Motor Supply had failed to keep adequate records of hours worked and pay time-and-a-half for hours in excess of 40 per week.

By now, E.P. was approaching 70 years of age and he wanted to start extracting cash from the partnership. The partnership agreements had always provided that the entire right, title, and interest in the trade name Arnold Motor Supply, as well as the good-will of the business was owned entirely by E.P. The partnership agreed to purchase the name and good-will of Arnold Motor Supply for $400,000 payable to E.P. in monthly installments. This agreement provided E.P. with income should he wish to retire, and provided the partnership with the assurance of business continuity in the event of E.P.'s death.

With the Department of Labor case still underway in federal court there was more drama happening within the company. E.P. loved the farm for his entire life. Where some men find relaxation with a golf club or fishing pole, E.P. wanted to unwind on the seat of a tractor or working with his prize Angus cattle. Across the street from the Merrill Company warehouse was an old welding shop the company used for excess storage. E.P. also used this building to house seed corn, fertilizer, and other farm supplies.

For years, E.P. had been in the habit of buying a new white Cadillac every year. He was so entrenched in this habit that one year when he found no white Cadillac was immediately available, he purchased one in another color and had it painted white. In the spring of the year you could count on E.P. to take out the back seat of his Cadillac, pull up across from the warehouse, and load the car with seed corn, weed killer, or fertilizer to drive down to his farm. Spectators would be amused by the Cadillac, its back end weighed down with farm supplies.

Some of the partners were not pleased that E.P. used warehouse space for farm related items. In reality, there was plenty of room and this practice caused no hardship to the partnership, but it did create resentment among a few that E.P. was using partnership resources for his personal farm. This resentment came to a head when the sale of trade name and good-will occurred at a price that some felt was too high. Chief among those objecting was Kieth Byers and his nephew Don. E.P. had recently installed several grain silos on the farm. Kieth, Don, and perhaps other partners suspected that E.P. had paid for the silos with partnership money and leveled this accusation against him.

In reality the purchases were made from a personal account, which he was able to prove by producing cancelled checks. E.P. was livid at the accusation and the confrontation he had with his accusers was the only time employees recall seeing or hearing him visibly angry. He slammed the checks down on the desk in Kieth's office, pointed an angry finger across the room and shouted, "don't ever call me a liar again!" With that he turned, stormed out the door, and the issue was not publicly spoken of again.

Despite proof of the legitimacy of the payments, Kieth and Don were still not pleased with the amount E.P. was to be paid by the partnership for the trade name. Since E.P. no longer owned the rights to Arnold Motor Supply, Kieth and Don felt that the partnership should move on without him. Kieth and Don were anxious to have E.P. step down from leadership because they felt they should be the ones to take control of the company. E.P. objected to this plan on two counts. First, he was not ready to completely step down, and second he felt that neither Kieth nor Don would be able to effectively lead the entire organization.

Kieth called a partnership meeting and the partners met in nearby Storm Lake without E.P. present to discuss the future of the partnership. Kieth consulted a lawyer who drew up a document listing requests to present to E.P. The document asked E.P. to turn over all tax information, bank records, and other documents regarding the partnership. The majority of the partners found themselves in the middle of an unwanted battle between Kieth and Don Byers on one side and E.P. Arnold on the other.

A small group left the Storm Lake meeting to drive to Spencer, intending to resolve the confrontation. Ray and

Gib Pullen, Gar Odor, Harvey McVey, and John Schnurr met with Kieth, Don, and E.P in what Harvey would call a "horrible, horrible meeting." E.P. was adamant that he would not turn over any of the requested documents, and he would not relinquish control of the company to Kieth or Don.

With his controlling interest withdrawn from Arnold Motor Supply, E.P. knew the partners could decide to side with Kieth and force him out. He spoke with some partners he knew would be loyal to him and moved their partnership equity from Arnold Motor Supply to The Merrill Company. As a result, he ensured The Merrill Company would have sufficient capital to continue operations completely independent of Arnold Motor Supply. This also increased the likelihood that he would remain in control of The Merrill Company should the partners oust him from management of Arnold Motor Supply.

E.P. presented the partners with two options. First, he suggested that Kieth and Don be allowed to stay in the company with Kieth stepping down from his General Manager position to be a supervisor over all 13 stores and Don moving from his job as manager in Boone to manage the Storm Lake store. Gar Odor would be promoted from Ames manager to General Manager, with E.P. to stay on and help provide guidance for Gar as long as his health would permit.

The second option was for E.P. to step down from all involvement with Arnold Motor Supply, move his office and that of the bookkeepers to The Merrill Company warehouse and leave the management of Arnold Motor Supply completely up to the discretion of the partners. He reminded the partners that he had founded the enterprise, led it through its growth and development, and admitted them all as partners after the business was well established.

Most partners agreed with E.P.'s assessment that Kieth and Don would not be able to effectively run the organization. Most were also loyal to E.P. and were not about to force him to step down. Realizing that he could no longer effectively supervise stores after what some perceived as a mutiny against E.P., Kieth called Ray Pullen on April 20, 1968 to tender his resignation. He left his keys on his desk, went to the bank to take his name off the signature card and parted ways with his brother-in-law and the company he had been a part of for 37 years.

Ray Pullen, heeding E.P.'s suggestion of Gar for the new General Manager, sent a memo to the 35 Arnold Motor Supply senior partners on April 26 saying, "Under the circumstances of the past two weeks, I feel we should make our appointment of a new General Manager as soon as possible." He went on to recommend Gar for this position and asked for a vote from each senior partner. The results were mixed but ultimately Gar was approved.

Don Byers was only 47 years old and was in no financial position to quit his job. He still felt he could run a company and decided to go on his own to form an auto parts business that would compete with Arnold Motor

Supply. He began to actively recruit Arnold Motor Supply employees to work for him, convincing several from his store in Boone. He then purchased land for a store. Word of his plans got back to Spencer, and he and seven others were fired.

The naming of Gar as General Manager, Kieth's resignation, and the removal of Don Byers ended what had been a tumultuous spring of 1968. Nearly a year later, on May 6, 1969, the company got some welcome good news when the Department of Labor decided there was no criminal intent in the Fair Labor Standards Act case and it was promptly dismissed.

Through the first forty years of Arnold Motor Supply, there had been many ups and downs and constant challenges but the past three years had seen internal turmoil unmatched in any other period of company history. E.P. felt Arnold Motor Supply emerged from the 1960s with a solid foundation to move forward into the future. Gar Odor was prepared to lead the company into the 1970s under the watchful eye of Mr. Arnold.

Merrill, Irene, and E.P. Arnold in 1969

16. Sunset

Personally, Mr. Arnold paid a painful price for the position the company occupied on his 70th birthday. The union deliberations of 1966 had exhausted him and placed a lot of stress both on him and Irene. The developments with Kieth two years later cost E.P. a business partner and Irene a brother. Kieth and Irene would hardly speak for the next ten years after the split.

The first major event under Gar's leadership was the addition of a new store in Fort Dodge, Iowa. The 14th Arnold Motor Supply opened in December, 1970 with Larry Wegner as manager. In 1972, The Merrill Company expanded with the creation of a second Merrill Company warehouse in Marshalltown, Iowa to provide better service to the nine stores on the eastern half of the territory.

E.P. was impressed with Gar's management ability, saying "In watching Gar Odor work I believe he is one of the best organizers of people that I have ever seen." Mr. Arnold would frequently visit stores for special events, appear in radio interviews, and was the public face of Arnold Motor Supply. He was no mere figurehead, however. He continued to come to work every day and was actively involved in the bookkeeping functions of the company.

His philosophy and presence in the office continued to provide quiet guidance for the company.

In the early 1970s, while the nation was focusing on the Watergate scandal and Vietnam, Arnold Motor Supply was poised for expansion, again adding stores every other year. In 1972, the company acquired M & L Auto Parts in Ankeny, sending Gary Cleghorn there to manage the new location in October. Gary was a member of a growing second generation of the Arnold Motor Supply family. His father Lorol had joined the company in 1943 and Gary literally grew up with Arnold Motor Supply. As children, he and his brother had come to the store in the evenings to help, or perhaps hinder, their father as he loaded up his truck for the next day's sales route.

In 1974, the company purchased Sitler Auto Parts with stores in Fairfield and Washington, Iowa and sent Bob Loban to manage both locations. In 1976, Graff Auto Parts of Worthington, Minnesota was added to the growing Arnold Motor Supply chain which now numbered eighteen stores. All of the 1970s acquisitions were in buildings that were not up to Mr. Arnold's standards and by the end of the decade all had been moved to new locations.

As 1977 arrived, the organization was embarking on its 50th year and plans were in the works for a 50th Anniversary celebration. His friend of 45 years, Louis Goldberg wrote a tribute to Mr. Arnold which was printed in the program for the event. "Fifty years ago, a young man had an old car and some pieces of motor supplies. He also had a dream and a will to work and a dedication to duty. Today that dream is very real, very much alive. We see it all about us, in concrete form: Land and buildings and a mountain of motor supplies. We see it, moreover, in human form: in the 150 dedicated men and women who are partners in this Arnold Industrial empire. For the young man who had the dream did more than build a business: by example and by quiet guidance he also helped to build dedicated men and women."

Louis Goldberg was very perceptive and concise. In six sentences he managed to put on paper the essence of Mr. Arnold and his fifty years with Arnold Motor Supply. E.P. Arnold did indeed have a dream in 1927, along with the work ethic and perseverance to see his dream through. Goldberg realized, as E.P. did, that the people of the company were the real fulfillment of the dream, not buildings or assets or inventories. E.P. had built the company, and built the dream by building up people. He built people not by boisterous promises nor by intimidation but by kind, firm guidance and example.

The 50th Anniversary celebration, held on Saturday April 2, 1977 was the opportunity for all the partners Mr. Arnold had affected over the years to say "thank you" to the man they respected. It was the grand finale to the story of E.P. Arnold. In 1927, he had launched the company behind the wheel of a 1927 Chevrolet Roadster. The car symbolized the superior service that had differentiated Arnold Motor Supply from its competition from day one. The partners, all familiar with the story of the company's origin, decided a restored Roadster was the perfect thank you present.

Jerry Poock, Merrill Company warehouse manager, located a 1928 Roadster in Hardy, Nebraska. The partnership purchased the car, loaded it on a truck and brought it back to Spencer where it was secretly restored over the next several months. When finished, it was a near exact replica of the original car E.P. had driven on his sales route, complete with the wooden box he had built on the back to carry his inventory of parts. It was an emotional moment when the business meeting concluded and the car was driven from behind the curtain and presented to Mr. Arnold.

The celebration was Mr. Arnold's final large scale interaction with the company he loved. The Arnold family was now facing personal health struggles. E.P. was diagnosed with Parkinson's disease, which gradually stole his mobility and left him unable to continue his daily involvement with the company. At the same time, Merrill was diagnosed with brain cancer and taken to the Mayo Clinic in Rochester, Minnesota. When the Worthington store celebrated its new building with a Grand Opening celebration in October, 1977 Mr. Arnold was absent. He wrote a greeting, which he asked Gar to read, and apologized for being unable to attend in person due to "illness in our own family." In November, E.P. himself was taken to the Mayo Clinic in Rochester in critical condition.

Merrill's brain tumor proved to be inoperable. By the end of 1977, both Mr. Arnold and Merrill were back in Spencer where they were admitted to a nursing home to receive full-time care. In January, Mr. Arnold took a turn for the worse. He was transferred to the Spencer Hospital, which he had played a significant role in building twelve years earlier. A few partners were able to visit him on his last day of life to say their goodbyes. E.P. Arnold passed away on January 9, 1978. Gar sent a message to all stores notifying them that they had lost their founder. Irene wanted a small private funeral for her husband of fifty-four years. Warner Funeral Home, in the beautiful brick English Tudor home the Arnolds had built over forty years earlier, was the site of the funeral service. Three months later Merrill passed away on April 8 at the age of 45.

E.P. Arnold with the restored Roadster at the 50th Anniversary

17. Direction

Gar Odor proved to be a very capable manager over the first ten years of his tenure as General Manager. The OPEC oil embargo of 1973 led to a challenging time in the automotive aftermarket. Arnold Motor Supply steered through this time with continued growth. As long as Mr. Arnold was alive to provide the high-level vision for the company, Gar was proficient at executing that vision. Once Mr. Arnold passed away, the true test of his leadership began.

The first major event of this period was the addition of a new store in LeMars, Iowa. True to the pattern established from the beginning, LeMars was the county seat of Plymouth County, with a population of just over 8,000. Located 70 miles southwest of Spencer and 40 miles from the closest Arnold Motor Supply in Sheldon, LeMars was the exact type of location Mr. Arnold would have chosen for the nineteenth store.

At the dawn of the 1980s, the landscape of the industry was shifting. Just as independent stores had faced massive competition from chain stores in the late 1950s and 1960s, the 1970s brought stiff competition to independent warehouses. In order to compete with the high degree of buying power these national chains enjoyed, it was obvious warehouse distributors who wished to remain independent must join forces to buy and market products cooperatively. These organized groups of independent warehouse distributors were referred to as Program Groups since they would join forces to create a single marketing program.

The National Auto Parts Association, today known as NAPA began its nationwide growth through mergers and acquisitions during the 1970s. Bumper to Bumper was founded in 1973 by Martin Brown of Kansas City, Missouri. In 1974, O. Temple Sloan of General Parts Inc. of North Carolina joined forces with two other warehouse distributors to form CARQUEST. In order to compete with other large retailers, both NAPA and CARQUEST continued to expand into new territories by acquiring or merging with existing warehouse distributors. The program group All Pro was founded in 1976 by Riley Taylor, Sr. of Andalusia, Alabama.

Also in 1976, Dick Downey of Chattanooga, Tennessee, Bill Cherry of Nashville, Tennessee, Herman Siegel of Birmingham, Alabama and Jack Alexander of Atlanta, Georgia decided they would retain an antitrust lawyer to create the charter of Auto Value Associates. With Dick Downey as chairman, Auto Value buying group set out to provide combined purchasing power and shared marketing programs for its member distribution companies.

Gar and a group of partners met with Downey and Auto Value representatives to discuss how The Merrill

Company could benefit from joining the other warehouse distributors in the association. It was decided this step was essential to the continued growth of the company. On March 14, 1983, The Merrill Company was one of the first distributors to join the original four Auto Value Associates shareholding members.

As the company moved into the last half of the decade, there was growing discontent with Gar's leadership inside the company. Partners felt problems in Gar's personal life were affecting his work performance. Some of his decisions did not mesh well with the culture of the company, and there was disagreement with his vision for the future. As a result, morale within the partnerships reached an all-time low. Long- time Arnold Motor Supply partners began to question the wisdom of leaving their money in the partnership.

Managers in the fall of 1986

From the very beginning, the company had been in a state of perpetual growth. Growth was part of the vision. Whether adding new locations or constructing new buildings, the company had always been in the middle of an expansion project or planning the next one. Mr. Arnold's focus had been on building a company and he made decisions optimized for long- term success. After joining Auto Value, Gar seemed to completely lose that focus. Instead of building for long-term growth and sustainability, Gar felt that selling Arnold Motor Supply and The Merrill Company was the best path to pursue. As a result, his decisions became focused on increasing the short-term value of the organization in order to maximize the selling price rather than build the long-term stability of the company.

The direction Gar wanted to steer the partnerships was not the direction the partners wanted to go. Gar had been in contact with Temple Sloan of CARQUEST and discussed selling the partnerships. Sloan invited the senior partner group to the CARQUEST facility in Lakeville, Minnesota to discuss terms of sale. The partners were offered stock in CARQUEST in exchange for ownership of the Arnold Motor Supply stores and The Merrill Company. The partners were not willing to sell and they instructed Gar to break off discussions with Sloan. Gar insisted that the future of the company was with CARQUEST and would not relent.

Ultimately the partners called a meeting to determine if Gar would continue as General Manager. In September, 1990, the senior partners of Arnold Motor Supply and The Merrill Company met in Spencer to determine which direction the partnerships would take. Gar was asked to leave the room while the remaining partners discussed and then voted on retaining him as Managing Partner. While the vote was not unanimous, the partners overwhelmingly voted to remove Gar from leadership. Lawyers were brought in to negotiate his severance from the partnership. He remained confident in CARQUEST and went to work for Temple Sloan in North Carolina.

The partnerships now found themselves in unknown territory. Mr. Arnold and his handpicked successor Gar, had lead them through the first 63 years of existence. An interim management committee consisting of four store managers and a warehouse buyer was formed, but a company cannot be effectively run for long by a committee. It was obvious that someone would need to be named the new General Manager, but no single person stood out as an obvious choice.

18. Renewed Clarity

Those with interest in the General Manager position were asked to state their case before the senior partners. Several different managers from within the company made presentations. In January, four months after Gar was dismissed, the partners selected Ankeny store manager Milo Allen to assume the role of General Manager. Milo's vision for growth matched the vision of the partners who knew the company had become stagnant over the past decade due to lack of vision and poor leadership. With Milo's promotion, the attitude throughout the entire company changed almost overnight.

Milo knew that growth was the objective. That was the mandate of the partners who chose him. Unlike the early days of the company when growth could be accomplished by opening new locations, the business climate of the 1990s did not lend itself to building new stores. Rather, it made much more sense to bring existing independent stores into the organization. Arnold Motor Supply faced two challenges in the quest for growth through acquisition. First, they had to supply the cash flow to buy, and then they had to convince independent owners to join Arnold Motor Supply.

Milo's first task was increasing cash available for expansion, a sizable amount of which would have to come from within the partnership. Partners needed to agree to take a smaller percentage of the profits out of the business in the form of compensation and bonuses and instead reinvest money back into the company to increase the cash flow. This increased cash helped prepare the way for expansion.

A better relationship with bankers was also necessary to secure the required financing. The company needed a larger line of credit to fulfill the plans for growth. Since the most important asset of Arnold Motor Supply and The Merrill Company has always been people, it made sense to introduce bankers to the company in a way they are not used to seeing clients. After a less-than-fruitful meeting with loan officers, Milo proposed they leave the bank, financial statements, and paper work and instead take a tour of the Arnold Motor Supply stores. The bankers agreed. After seeing the stores in operation, meeting the people of the partnership, and gaining a better understanding of what Arnold Motor Supply stood for, the bankers were more receptive to the plans Milo laid out and agreed to the financing that was required.

With the financial foundation in place, attention turned to finding businesses to bring into the Arnold Motor Supply family. Milo would later say, "We already had enough inventory and buildings, we were looking to add good people." Arnold Motor Supply was not the only company courting these independent jobbers in the 1990s but Milo had a unique angle to convince them to come aboard.

Other potential purchasers would approach an independent store owner and try to convince him to sell. Instead, Milo would convince him to buy. He would talk up the partnership and the unique opportunities it provided and try to convince the independent owner to buy into the partnership. Arnold Motor Supply would take over ownership of the store but retain the owner and his people to run the business. This approach proved very successful and brought a tremendous influx of talented new people into the company. This philosophy and people-centric approach to acquisition allowed Arnold Motor Supply to expand from nineteen stores in 1991 to thirty seven stores only eight years later.

Managers in the fall of 1994

In 1996 Arnold Motor Supply was faced with the challenge of staffing all of the new stores and adding additional weekend hours to compete with retail oriented stores who were moving into the territory. This resulted in the need for part-time employees, which was difficult to accomplish when everyone was required to become a partner. The additional tax requirements of partnership and the investment requirement made it difficult to attract all the people the company needed. It was decided to change the structure of the partnership to once again allow for employees. All existing partners were given the choice to stay in the partnership or become employees. An invitation to join the partnership began to be extended to top performing employees on an annual basis.

In 1999, Milo announced the intention to take another large step forward. He had been talking to the owners of Specialty Sales Company, an auto parts warehouse in Omaha, Nebraska, which owned eleven stores across eastern Nebraska. In April, 1999 the Omaha warehouse plus these stores were added to the company, bringing the total number of parts stores to forty eight.

Milo would frequently attend seminars on business practices to help him grow as a leader and businessman. One of the things he heard in multiple seminars was the importance of finding and grooming a successor. Prior to his promotion to General Manager, Milo had been the store manager in Ankeny for many years. Dennis Spooner had started sweeping the floors in Ankeny and doing whatever needed to be done around the store. He moved up to work on the counter, then to sales. As salesman, Dennis served as Milo's right hand man, filling in whenever he was gone. When Milo moved up to be General Manager, Dennis was promoted to store manager.

Milo saw in Dennis the perfect characteristics to be the next General Manager. After six years of managing the store in Ankeny, Dennis was promoted to District Manager in 1997. In 2000, Dennis was promoted again. He moved to Spencer to assume the role of Operations Manager responsible for all store operations. The intent was to spend the next seven to eight years learning the warehouse and financial aspects of the company and then replace Milo as General Manager.

After the rapid explosion of growth through the past decade, the company needed to pause and catch its breath. The focus needed to shift, at least temporarily, away from adding locations to integrating these new locations into the fabric of the company and improving efficiencies within the organization. The Arnold Motor Supply way had always been to fill management positions from within. The new philosophy of bringing in managers with new stores resulted in a large set of people who had not been brought up within the culture of the company.

The rapid growth had stretched the organization to its limit financially and organizationally. The Omaha acquisition was costing more than anticipated and was putting a strain on the finances. Milo decided his strength was growing the company and it had grown as far as it could. The company needed a different type of leader, someone to take all the new pieces that had been added to the company and get them into the right roles doing the right things in the right way. Milo felt he should step out of the role of General Manager sooner than expected; a role he felt would now be a better fit for Dennis. Gary Cleghorn was retiring from the company and Milo wanted to move into his position of Inventory Manager. The partners agreed, and on March 1, 2002 they named Dennis Spooner the new General Manager.

19. The Path Forward

Just as Milo Allen had assumed the General Manager position with a vision and corresponding mandate for growth, Dennis stepped into the role with a vision and mandate as well. After the period of frenetic growth, the company needed to buckle down, focus on fundamentals and move forward as a unified and efficient organization. The first area of focus was reduction of debt. The company had pushed up against its line of credit during the rush to grow and now fiscal discipline was needed to ensure it would stay on a solid financial footing. In order to save on financing costs, the debt-to-equity ratio was targeted for reduction.

In order to reduce debt and still grow, Dennis instilled a vision to grow the company at a pace consistent with the financial commitment of the partners. Partners responded to this vision by putting more money into the partnership. By focusing on increased internal investment rather than external financing, the partnership was able to double the available capital for growth while reducing both short-term and long-term debt. This fiscal discipline was needed to ensure the growing company would stay on solid financial footing.

The new stores brought with them many capital needs, so physical plant expenditures needed more focus. They required a more disciplined approach to budgeting than had ever been necessary in the past. With the help of Steve Lensing, the company's Controller, income statements and budgets were analyzed for each of the different locations to help stores improve on areas where they were in need of more efficient operation.

Another area of focus was inventory. Any wholesale or retail organization is greatly affected by inventory turn, the number of times the average inventory amount is sold over the course of a year. A low inventory turn indicates the company has too much money tied up in inventory and may be buying the wrong items or too much quantity. A high inventory turn means there might not be enough inventory on hand to meet demand, which means potential sales are lost. An emphasis was placed on ensuring inventory levels were improved to minimize over-stocking and lost sales.

In any business, making a sale is important but collecting money from the sale is the final step to make the transaction profitable. Not only is it important to collect a high percentage of the money owed to you, it is also important to collect it quickly to provide cash flow to pay obligations of the organization. A ratio used to measure effectiveness of accounts receivable practices is days receivable, which divides the total amount receivable by the average sales per day. By placing a targeted effort on monitoring and adjusting credit limits and better collection practices, the company was able to significantly reduce days receivable, which provided more cash flow for growth.

The demographics in the company that resulted from the growth in previous decades led to a high number of partners at or near retirement age. Another area of focus was bringing down the ratio of retired partners to active partners, which would ensure enough young partners were investing in the company to provide equity to offset the current and projected expense of paying out to retired partners.

Finally, after addressing these foundational concerns, the company again turned its focus to growth. The target was now slow, sustainable growth and businesses were sought to bring into the company. The search was not constrained just to auto parts stores. Dennis was interested in adding any type of company that had synergies with the existing business. Moving into activities not directly related to selling auto parts would provide a level of diversification for the company. The beginning of this movement occurred in 1996 when the company formed a division called Light Industrial Coatings.

This new division, which sold paint and powder coatings to manufacturers, was a natural outflow of the automotive paint business the company had been involved with going all the way back to the 1930s. Many of the skills and knowledge required for selling and providing service to automotive paint customers translated very well into selling other kinds of coatings.

In 2003, the company purchased Industrial Paint Supply in Omaha, Nebraska. This addition fit the company very well. It was physically moved to share space with the Specialty Sales warehouse and its product offerings fit nicely with the Light Industrial Coatings division. Eventually these two entities were merged and renamed Industrial Paint Solutions.

More diversification came in 2005 when the company acquired Midwest Cylinder Head in Nevada, Iowa. This new division specialized in cast iron welding and remanufacturing of cylinder heads, engine blocks, crankshafts, and transmission housings. This division perfectly complemented the existing machine shop business in the stores and gave the company a manufacturing presence in contrast to its existing retail, wholesale, and distribution model.

Since Arnold Motor Supply already had relationships with a large number of body shop customers, the next move to diversify came in 2006 when the store in Sioux City, Iowa started selling and servicing spray booths and other equipment common to the body shop industry. From this division, the company continued to expand its product offerings by adding replacement panels for collision repair such as bumpers, fenders, hoods and mirrors.

During this period of slow and steady growth, sales nearly doubled during a ten year period. Because of the efforts to streamline operations and bring costs under control, the increase in sales resulted in record levels of success in multiple areas of the company's financial statements.

Through all of the shoring up, diversification, and steady growth of this period, the overarching focus was on people. The leadership of the company recognized the truth articulated by Mr. Arnold decades earlier: "You build a business with people."

Arnold Motor Supply in Spencer, Iowa

20. Lessons Learned

The story of E.P. Arnold and the company he founded is more than just interesting history. It is a case study of an American dream. America today is completely different from the America of a century ago, but the lessons that E.P. Arnold learned and the principles he applied through his career are timeless. The culture he established is still very real within Arnold Motor Supply and The Merrill Company. As the company reached its 85th year of business in 2012, thirty four years after his death, the partnerships still employed 24 people who were with the company for the 50th Anniversary celebration. These two dozen people provide a direct link to the legacy of Mr. Arnold.

It is human nature to try to formulate success, a trait that is both positive and negative. Success is not something that can be bottled and easily reproduced. It is certainly possible however to learn from success and by learning from it increase the likelihood of future success. What can be learned from Mr. Arnold and the history of his company?

The single most outstanding aspect of Arnold Motor Supply and The Merrill Company is the concept of partnership. In Mr. Arnold's own words, "I have believed that a Partnership was the best way to set up a business so that all parties involved furnished capital and services and that they all shared in net profits." Partnership is far more than just the legal organization of the company.

Over its history, Arnold Motor Supply has been structured as a Corporation, a General Partnership, and a Limited Liability Partnership. Despite the legal differences, the principle was always the same. Mr. Arnold was adamant that employees have a vested interest in the company, believing that they would work harder and care more, which would, of course, make the company more likely to succeed. The key is that everyone must believe that what happens corporately to the company really does directly affect them personally.

When Mr. Arnold started Arnold Motor Supply he was one of many young entrepreneurs in the area trying to make a name for himself in business. Few, if any, of the businesses began by his contemporaries have grown into multi-million dollar enterprises the way his did. By sharing ownership and profits, he made a calculated decision to maximize long-term income by sharing early profits and opening up partnership opportunities. Doing so attracted better people, which made a better company. In the long run, this made him and his company more successful.

Credit for establishment of the partnership has to be shared with Mr. Arnold's longtime friend and attorney Louis S. Goldberg. Mr. Goldberg established his law practice in Sioux City, Iowa in 1926 and acted not only as

Mr. Arnold's legal counsel but also as his CPA. Mr. Goldberg wrote several articles for publication in law journals, using his background as both lawyer and accountant to help lawyers understand the principles of accounting. Just as Mr. Arnold's association with B.J. Lewis was key to the formation of the company, his association with Louis Goldberg was key to the formation of the partnership.

From its inception, Arnold Motor Supply stood for exceptional customer service. The 1927 Chevrolet Roadster represented the first effort to deliver parts better and more quickly than anyone else. In the 1950s, Mr. Arnold articulated his focus on service, "We believe price is not of importance – someone will always undersell us – but we believe our service is of importance. We believe our responsibility is first to our customers, the sole reason for our existence; then to our employees whom we depend on to serve those customers; and then to the ownership or partners."

In 1999, the Auto Value program group that The Merrill Company joined in 1983 merged with All Pro/Bumper to Bumper, another successful program group. The newly formed organization known as The Aftermarket Auto Parts Alliance was incorporated on January 1, 2000 and held its first joint meeting that December. The Alliance later developed a marketing strategy around the slogan "Service is the Difference."

For Arnold Motor Supply, "Service is the Difference" is not simply a strategy or slogan, it is an identity. To be truly effective, any marketing program has to go beyond a slogan to become reality. Putting "Service is the Difference" bumper stickers on delivery trucks does not make it so. Only when the people driving the trucks accept it and live it will the customers believe it. It has been said there is no success without a succession. The excellent service provided today by a new employee born years after Mr. Arnold's death is the biggest evidence of his success as a leader and visionary.

21. Traits of a Leader

Forming a partnership focused on service was a wise decision, but it would not have succeeded without the traits that Mr. Arnold possessed personally and infused into the organization. What was it about Mr. Arnold that propelled him and his company to succeed where many others could not? Over the years, there are common threads running through the life of E.P. individually and as a result, Arnold Motor Supply corporately. These threads of leadership are vision, people, character, and attitude.

In his book *The 21 Irrefutable Laws of Leadership,* author John C. Maxwell points out the importance of a good leader at the head of an organization, "People buy into the leader before they buy into the vision." This was certainly true for Mr. Arnold. Those who worked for him held him in the highest regard. Bob Black, long- time shop man reflected on Mr. Arnold in 2002 saying, "The one thing we had to do was treat the customer with respect. If you made a customer mad, you had the whole outfit on you, especially Mr. Arnold. I still call him Mr. Arnold out of respect for him. He's been dead for twenty years but you still respect him."

The earliest employee of Arnold Motor Supply, Florence Rusch shared her thoughts of Mr. Arnold, calling him, "a very nice boss, a wonderful boss, a person who was concerned about other people." Those who worked for Mr. Arnold trusted him and knew that he cared about their individual and collective success. Mr. Arnold was a true leader who was able to inspire his people to follow the vision he put before them.

Of course, having people willing to follow does no good if there is no clear vision of where to lead them. The book of Proverbs correctly says, "Where there is no vision the people perish." No organization can thrive without a well-defined vision. Mr. Arnold said it this way, "I believe any business should have a creed or things in which it believes." He articulated his vision for meeting the needs of customers through superior service. He communicated this vision both with his words and his actions.

Once Mr. Arnold had placed the vision before the company, his expectations were unwavering. He would not hesitate to correct anyone in the company who did not live up to the high standards he set. When correction came, it did not come in the form of belittlement or public berating. Correction was firm and clear but also consistent and considerate. He would plainly point out how things had to be and would also explain why they had to be that way.

When he took the reigns as General Manager in 2002, Dennis Spooner wrote an article in the company newsletter in which he said, "Customer service is why we are here

155

and auto parts are just what we sell along the way. We are in the needs business - generally our customers NEED to buy a part. Therefore it is our job to make our customers feel special. Give them your undivided attention and show them you will go out of your way to help them out. Show them you care. Our company was founded by this commitment."

Forty-four years before Dennis wrote these words for the newsletter, E.P. Arnold told an interviewer, "Ours is a service business, and we've been successful because we are always ready to provide emergency service. We never refuse to open our stores. We've followed this policy for 30 years- our customers know it and depend on it." Seventy-five years after the formation of the company, the original vision was still intact, unaltered, and leading the way forward. Arnold Motor Supply has existed nearly as long after the death of Mr. Arnold as it did during his life. The culture of the company today is a powerful example of the importance of vision and the effect it can have long after the leader is gone.

In the words of Theodore Roosevelt, "People don't care how much you know until they know how much you care." Putting people ahead of profits from the beginning had the effect of maximizing both. Mr. Arnold placed a high value on his people and expected them to place a high value on customers, vendors, and anyone else the company was associated with. Even when the company had grown to 18 stores across two states Mr. Arnold still thought of every customer as his own. He would say,

"These are my customers and I want these customers treated right."

When faced with increasing competition from national chains AutoZone and O'Reilly's in the 1990s, the company proclaimed that its competitive strategy hinged on its people. The philosophy Mr. Arnold established within the company was based on the premise that people buy from people. From that foundation, hiring and retaining the best people possible and empowering them to meet the needs of customers is the best way to compete with anyone. It has been said the most valuable resources any company has are its human resources. It is the people, empowered by the leadership and the vision that make the difference.

What was the ingredient that let Mr. Arnold be such an effective visionary leader of people? He was neither an imposing physical specimen nor a dynamic, charismatic speaker. He did not speak loudly but he spoke with an authority born of character. John C. Maxwell says, "It's true that charisma can make a person stand out for a moment, but character sets a person apart for a lifetime." Because Mr. Arnold acted with character, he developed trust with his people and that trust was the foundation of his leadership.

No person is perfect and no company can be perfect either, but character was a foundational principle of Mr. Arnold and the company he conceived. It is character that dictates how a company will respond when a vendor ships more product than they bill for. It is character that determines how an employee will react when presented with the opportunity to pocket money. Character ultimately defines how an organization operates.

It is character that flows down from leadership that sets the tone for the organization. When discussing what Mr. Arnold saw as important in an employee, Bob Black suggested, "always be honest, honesty was the most important thing." You can't underestimate importance of character in a leader. If the leadership of any organization does not operate in integrity the entire organization is going to suffer.

Of the attributes that define the culture of an organization, attitude is perhaps the most immediately tangible. When you walk into a store, the attitude of the employees is really the first thing you see. It may be visible through the way stock is presented on the shelves or how clean the floor is, but these are simply indicators of the attitudes in the store. There is one thing definite about attitude, it is contagious. Mr. Arnold was known for an upbeat, can-do attitude. He was never about making "blue sky" promises or unrealistic projections, but in the face of any problem, he was able to continue to be optimistic for a solution.

Not only are attitudes visible, they can be felt. A group of people with a good attitude is a pleasure to be around and a pleasure to do business with. Since the Arnold Motor Supply adage of "people buy from people" is true, attitude has been an integral piece of the success of the company. All things being equal, a good attitude wins. In fact, frequently even if all things are not equal, a good attitude can overcome other disadvantages and still win.

158

When James Truslow Adams and Mark Twain were writing about the American Dream a century ago, E.P. Arnold was exactly the type of man they were writing about. Twain warned that the dream which drives men toward some chosen point was sometimes dangerous because the point was sometimes badly chosen. In the case of Ervin Phillip Arnold, his dream was well chosen.

Whether he could have imagined the company growing to be as large as it is today is debatable. What is certain is that the risks he took following his vision and going into business on his own back in 1927 paid off handsomely for him and the over 3,000 men and women who have depended on his company over the years for their livelihoods. Today, the legacy of Mr. Arnold lives on in the people who make up the company he founded.

Portrait of E.P. Arnold presented in 1967

Bibliography

Adams, J. T. (1931). *The Epic of America*. Boston: Little, Brown and Company.

Humphrey, P. (. (1995). *America in the 20th Century*. New York: Marshall Cavendish.

Maxwell, J. C. (1998). *The 21 Irrefutable Laws of Leadership*. Nashville: Thomas Nelson.

Parker Historical Society of Clay County. (1984). *The History of Clay County, Iowa*. Dallas: Curtis Media Corporation.

Ross, E. D. (1942). *A History of Iowa State College*. Ames: Iowa State College Press.

Sage, L. L. (1974). *A History of Iowa*. Ames, IA: The Iowa State University Press.

Schmidt, J. (2006). *Conflagration*. Spencer, IA: Spencer Alliance for a Creative Economy.

Schoffner, P. (2008). *History of the Iowa Automobile Dealers Association*. Des Moines: The Iowa Automobile Dealers Association.

Shapiro, G. (2011). *The Comeback*. New York: Beaufort Books.

Twain, M., & Warner, C. D. (1873). *The Gilded Age*. Hartford: American Publishing Company.